Unwomanly
Conduct

Unwomanly Conduct

The Challenges of Intentional Childlessness

Carolyn M. Morell

Routledge · New York & London

Published in 1994 by

Routledge
29 West 35th Street
New York, NY 10001

Published in Great Britain by

Routledge
11 New Fetter Lane
London EC4P 4EE

Library of Congress Cataloging-in-Publication Data

Morell, Carolyn M. (Carolyn Mackelcan), 1942–
    Unwomanly conduct : the challenges of intentional childlessness /
Carolyn M. Morell.
        p.   cm.
    Includes bibliographical references and index.
    ISBN 0-415-90677-6   ISBN 0-415-90678-4 (pbk.)
    1. Childlessness—Psychological aspects. 2. Women—Psychology.
3. Feminist theory.   I. Title.
HQ760.M67   1994
305.42—dc20   93-45984
                                                          CIP

For
Carol M. Morell
Jean Garis Flood & Harold D. Flood
and to the memory of
Elgin D. Morell

CONTENTS

ACKNOWLEDGMENTS

RESEARCH and writing demand many lonely hours, but the process depends upon the involvement of others. Over the past seven years many individuals have supported my work. My first debt is to the women who consented to be interviewed, giving me their time and their stories. Their courage and resourcefulness sustain me in a very personal way.

At the dissertation stage, my director and mentor, Carole Joffe, provided overarching support for my research. I am grateful for the skillful guidance she provided from the very beginning. Carole encouraged me to choose a topic that was "personally compelling" since she correctly anticipated I was in for a long haul. Throughout the process she treated me as a scholar in my own right and critiqued my ideas without imposing her own. Carole was available to me in a dedicated way whenever I needed her.

Thank you to Leslie Alexander for her enthusiastic support, and her willingness to sit on my dissertation committee. I also want to thank other members of my committee—Jane Caplan, Lenard Kaye, Jane Goodale, and Cynthia Brownstein. I also thank Diane Craw for her warmth and technical assistance.

On the home front, Larry Flood extended himself to me in a daily and dependable way that defies belief. He participated in unrelenting conversations about childlessness, read and edited, helped with research tasks and generally placed himself "on call" to assist me. I appreciate the tolerance he developed for haphazard living in the domestic realm. And I am grateful for the interest he takes in my scholarly endeavors.

My mother, Carol Morell, and my sister, Margaret Campbell, were wonderful supports throughout these years. Both scouted out women for me to interview. While sitting in my sister's kitchen one holiday I remember her asking, "How many more interviews do we need?" My mother always had words of great wisdom and compassion that helped keep me going during periods of doubt and tedium. She supported me in a myriad of material and metaphysical ways. On periodic visits "home," her sofa became my wintertime hang-out and the beautiful yard my summertime haven. Both Carol and Margaret are Christian Science practitioners and I consider each of them my "teacher" and "friend." I also thank my cousin, Linda Hilliard, who helped identify participants and provided several days of hospitality while I conducted interviews.

Jean Garis Flood and The Reverend Harold D. Flood have been enthusiastic supporters throughout the years. In the early stages of this project, I was living away from my partner and near the Floods. Regular escapes from my graduate student residence to the Flood household provided needed home-cooked meals, a comfortable place to nap, and a serene, affectionate atmosphere. My mind benefitted, as well as my body, by our frequent visits. I appreciated our many involved conversations about poetry, writing, and living a life that serves and gratifies.

Many friends and colleagues were there when I needed them. Early on, Barbara Simon's belief that the experiences of childless women were worthy of feminist and social work theorizing provided important validation. In the middle stages, the Graduate Group for Feminist Studies at the University of Buffalo gave me helpful encouragement. A special thank you to Liz Kennedy for her critical assessment of my theoretical claims and her ongoing interest in my work. Women attending my workshop at the National Association of Women in Psychology also offered validation and insights. I thank the social workers attending my presentation at the 6th National Symposium on Doctoral Research and Social Work Practice for their excitement about my methodology. It is important to me to have recognition from my profession for a rather unconventional social work approach.

I offer thanks to all those who have in some way supported this effort. While it is impossible to name every person, I want to identify at least a few: Michelle Fine, Marcia Hill, Ann Snitow, Laura Salwen, June Licence, Joan Levine, John B. Stranges, Susan Mason, Lou LaBarber, Mary Ann Deibel-Braun, Marge Fura, Laura Grube, Mary Hobgood, Jeanne Phoenix Laurel, Jean Richardson, Doug Koritz, Terry McDonough, Janet Meiselman, Susan Biller, and Jo Marie Privitera. Thanks to the women in my dinner group and to my potluck family who all helped me to keep going. Also, thanks to Chris Dietz and Shirley Lord, companion steering committee members of the Western New York chapter of the Bertha Capen Reynolds Society (a national organization of progressive social workers), for their interest and friendship.

A Women's Studies Fellowship from the Woodrow Wilson National Foundation and the Rivitz Award from the faculty of the Bryn Mawr College Graduate School of Social Work and Social Research made full-time work on this project possible in the early stages. For the Rivitz award I am indebted to Maurice Sall who established the fellowship in memory of his daughter, Joan Sall Rivitz. Niagara University has supported my scholarly activities by awarding course load reductions.

A version of the "Troubling Developments" chapter was published in the Fall, 1993 issue of *Affilia: Journal of Women and Social Work*. And a version of my preface was printed in Irene Reti's excellent collection of essays, *Childless by Choice: A Feminist Anthology,* which appeared in 1992. I appreciate the editorial assistance and confirmation that I received from both publishing opportunities.

Final and important words of gratitude go to the many workers at Routledge. No writer could ask for a nicer group of people to work with. I feel very fortunate to have Cecelia Cancellaro as my editor. From the start, she guided this project in a highly adept fashion, offering needed technical and moral support at every turn. I often talked with Cecelia's editorial assistant, Maura Burnett, who was generous with her time and also provided me with effective, helpful assistance. Michael J. Esposito managed the production of the book brilliantly. I appreciate their warmth and competence.

PREFACE:
A RESEARCHER'S STORY

ONE of the distinctive features of feminist inquiry is insistence that the researcher appear "not as an invisible, anonymous voice of authority, but as a real, historical individual with concrete, specific desires and interests."[1] The reader should know that I am a European–American woman in my fifties, married, middle-class, and I come to the subject of this book with my own history as an intentionally childless woman. I have strong identifications as a social worker, a feminist, a political activist.

Women who choose to remain childless share a common social context but we do not all react to that context in the same way. Some women seem to be impervious to popular beliefs about not–mothering women as incomplete, as inadequate, as having inferior lives. One woman I interviewed put it this way, "you have to understand, Carolyn—childlessness—it's just not in my head." Unfortunately (and fortunately for my research) I have been susceptible to the dominant cultural constructions of childlessness. For me, being childless requires a measure of courage, as a personal journal entry can attest:

5/20/87: Visit to Dr. G. to get my back aligned. He asked what my dissertation topic was—I told him intentionally childless women. Big mistake. He said in so many words childless women are: tense, very tense; prone to worry as they get older (don't like going out of their houses); become isolated as they age; nuns are especially tense; career women become too self-absorbed; it's an unnatural way to live. He makes it a game to "guess" about his female patients before he looks at their card. He can usually tell the childless ones.

Frontal assaults like this one sting. Not all cultural communications are direct attacks. Some messages appear more "liberal," allowing of reproductive difference. But I remain sensitive to the pronatalism that is often subtly promoted. An example is a newspaper article I came across in 1987 titled, "Private Lives: Saying 'No' to Kids, Some Couples Find a Twosome Is Quite Enough." The article was written by a woman I respect. She is a reporter who has done a great deal to promote the welfare of the less powerful in the Buffalo area. In no way intended to be insensitive, the way the *Buffalo News* covered the story did not empower me as a woman without children.

Rather than the article standing alone on the page, highlighted just beneath it appears the author's story. Her autobiographical statement is framed by a black border and is printed on a background of light red ink. The headline reads: "For Her It Was Love, Marriage, Family:"

> Now that I know the insistent demands of babies and young children; the light hand needed in guiding teen-agers without stifling them, I understand why career couples hesitate to add a family to their lives . . . I also realize how naive—and blessed—we were in becoming parents and also how grateful I am that I don't have to struggle with the decision, which has turned out to be both the most demanding— and rewarding—thing I've done with my life.[2]

So much for childlessness as a viable option. I don't think this kind of juxtaposition would occur with other issues. Imagine a human interest article about gays and lesbians that on the same page features a statement by the heterosexual author promoting heterosexuality and expressing her gratitude for being a heterosexual. Whether ill- or well-intentioned, common discourses on childlessness are disturbing.

As I experience the status, being childless means simultaneously to be reminded of your second-rate life and to be ignored. As I grew into my middle years I went to the midlife literature for information and inspiration. What I found is that writers and researchers simply assume all adult women are mothers. Characteristics of the research included: few samples of childless women, lack of comparison between women with and without children,[3] and general lack of attention to intragender diversity.

The very definitions of midlife erase not–mothering women. Lillian Rubin, who wrote *Women of a Certain Age: The Midlife Search for Self,* defines midlife not as a stage tied to chronological age but as the post-parental years, "the point in the life cycle of the family when children are grown and gone, or nearly so."[4] And in *In Her Prime: A New View of Middle-Aged Women,* Judith K. Brown devises her own meaning: "Middle-age women (matrons) are women who have adult offspring and who are not yet frail or dependent."[5] According to these definitions, I am not a middle-aged woman. I certainly am not a middle-aged man. My midlife crisis suffers a perverse twist.

As I age I have many questions and few answers. Many of the predictable patterns that may fit the experience of mothers do not fit me. For example, the common notion of an "empty nest" has no application to my life. Have I never or always experienced this problem? In fact the characteristics and impact of my "nest" are different but there is no literature to characterize that difference. The experiences of not–mothering women have yet to be named. Our lives remain untheorized.

More accurately, our lives are under- and wrongly theorized. My comprehension of the consequences of being a childless woman increased while I was a doctoral student in Social Work and Social Research at Bryn Mawr College. From my not–mothering social location I continually confronted in my studies one of three assumptions: First, that adult women are mothers, an assumption that renders reproductive difference invisible; or second, that childless women do exist but our reproductive status is symptomatic of psychological or moral deficits; or third, the notion that childlessness, rather than evincing deficiency, is simply a "lifestyle choice." This last assumption, although the most friendly to not–mothers, remains problematic for me since the focus on lifestyle gives no evidence of a politics which I experience. Such a construction keeps the political safely personal, the social safely individual.

Many of the studies on childlessness I did discover, including the works of highly respected academics, not only pathologize my reproductive life but cause apprehension:

> Feminists like to point up the psychic costs for women of marriage and motherhood; but whereas the childless woman can never have a post-partum psychosis, being maternal may protect women—perhaps even narcissistic women—against the psychoses of *later* life.[6]

The authors of the above statement divide a psychiatric population of childless women into two categories, "aging tomboys" and "perpetual daughters." They perceive all childless women as remaining "disastrously vulnerable to the later life intimations of mortality" since they have never experienced "that great transformation of narcissism that renders the child's life more precious than their own." According to the authors, biological motherhood is so pivotal that those who never reproduce are likely to become "developmental casualties." *Developmental casualty*. Remaining childless is a constant test of perseverance.[7]

The feminist movement, a source of support throughout my adult life, also fails to validate reproductive difference. The strong public feminist voice of the early 1970s, arguing that women could have good lives without motherhood, is barely a whisper today. A maternal revivalism has occurred over the past two decades within feminism as well as in the dominant culture. As I read my books, journals, and newspapers, they suggest that motherhood is not only a good choice for women but the absolutely wonderful choice, indeed the only politically correct choice. I remember feeling very much like an outsider when in 1986 a late–timing pregnant woman appeared on the cover of *Ms.* with the headline: "When to Have Your Baby." The word "if" had vanished from feminist discussions of reproductive options.

In this highly personal fashion I discovered a research topic as a doctoral student. I had identified a gap in social science knowledge based on my own "felt experience" as an older not–mothering woman. As a feminist I felt unsupported. I decided I had to write the book I needed to read. I needed to hear the voices of other women without children and I needed a political analysis of those voices. I needed a feminist work that would attend to and promote reproductive diversity.

In summary, the work that follows cannot be considered independent of the person I present here. Given my history and identifications, I bring what I consider to be heightened sensitivities to the task which I hope deepen and enrich my analysis. I also understand, given the same history and set of allegiances, that there are blind spots that may cloud my inquiry into other childless women's lives. The usefulness of my contribution will be determined collectively through the social process of dialogue. My aim is to inject the voices of childless women into the discussions going on among feminists. Carolyn Heilbrun reminds me of the importance of becoming part of the conversation when she asserts: "The true representation of power is not a big man beating a smaller man or a woman. Power is the ability to take one's place in whatever discourse is essential to action and the right to have one's part matter."[8]

I

"Why aren't I being the hero?"
THE POLITICS OF REPRODUCTIVE DIFFERENCE

Why aren't I being the hero and why are younger women being so flaky and, I don't know, so "feminine" (Laughing). My choice is a valid one and it's never been discovered.

—Elaine, age 48

From the beginning, feminists set out to break two taboos: the taboo on describing the complex and mixed experiences of actual mothers and the taboo on the celebration of a child-free life. But for reasons both inside and beyond the women's movement, feminists were better able in the long run to attend to mothers' voices than they were able to imagine a full and deeply meaningful life without motherhood, without children.

—Ann Snitow[1]

OPTING to remain childless is barely imaginable for most women in the United States today. Throughout the culture, motherhood is celebrated while childlessness is promoted as a sorry state. Women without children are ignored unless they are desperately seeking motherhood or are regretfully watching others become mothers and grandmothers. Who is talking about women having viable lives without children of their own? Not many.[2]

The social promotion of motherhood, combined with criticism and inattention to the lives of not–mothering women, reinforces certain expectations about women generally; women are expected to desire to become mothers and to do so, to be "relational" in orientation, to gain power and satisfaction through caring for others, to do their most important work in the family circle. Maternalism—the notion that femaleness is rooted in motherly qualities so that women must become mothers in order to realize themselves[3]—is a central feature of the most recent backlash against the economic and social gains women achieved in the 1970s.[4] Over the past two hundred years, this ideology has been a bedrock of capitalist patriarchal organization, justifying women's unpaid domestic labor and subordinating women as a social group.

Historically, it has fallen to feminism to respond to attempts to limit women's freedom. But during the past two decades feminists have been oddly silent about childlessness as a vital possibility. Ann Snitow asks why pronatalism flourishes with so little argument from feminists. She asserts that feminist culture has not produced "alluring images" or "thinkable identities" for the childless.[5]

Given the present state of affairs, the overarching political project of this book is to undermine the beliefs which collapse the words "woman" and "mother." Several immodest and interrelated goals for this study suggest themselves. A first important goal is to commit to print the voices of women who are not mothers. We know little about the real consequences of remaining childless for adult women. Rarely is this group visible as a subject for feminist attention and analysis. I see the study, then, as a contribution to the ongoing feminist project of elucidating women's lives.

A second goal is to use the stories of childless women to critique cultural constructions of childlessness within and outside feminism to illuminate the culture of reproduction in which *all* women reside. Simply said, I want to raise consciousness about how the dominant culture naturalizes motherhood. And I want to offer respectful critiques of some contemporary feminist thought. Maternalism is pervasive within feminism and beyond, and it needs to be seen and acknowledged as such.

In this introductory chapter, I set the stage for later discussions by examining the European–American history of maternalist ideology and its present resurgence. I particularly focus on that strand of contemporary feminism that centers its analysis on motherhood. Next, I introduce the reader to my theoretical assumptions and methodological approach. After addressing issues of race and class, I end with the problem of language—the difficulty I experienced naming women who choose not to mother.

Maternalist Thinking: A Brief History

In the Beginning

There are women and there are ideas about women. While women themselves vary considerably, one idea about them seems stable: motherhood, as wish or reality, is their essential and defining characteristic or condition.

Beliefs, of course, are not independent of the social and historical conditions from which they spring. The middle-class, European–American view of womanhood that takes mothering as women's central work and identity developed with the rise of industrialization. The split between publicly organized production and privately organized reproduction and consumption was justified by a new ideology of motherhood and domesticity that posited a "natural" sexual division of labor.[6] Women were seen as possessing innate nurturant abilities and a moral purity that best fit them for work in the private sphere of the household, while men were understood to have independent and aggressive natures, well-suited to ruling in the public sphere.

Prior to the elevation of motherhood in the nineteenth century, raising children was integrated with other work women did. It was not considered their most important work, nor was it imbued with intense psychological significance:[7]

In a subsistence farm economy, survival required women as well as men place productive work before reproductive concerns. Women and men worked side by side, in and around the home. Women were responsible for food and clothing production for the family, which involved many complicated skills, as well as for cooking, laundering, cleaning, and childcare. Infants were tended when possible, and were sometimes played with, but were never the center of a mother's attention. Their care was largely the task of older siblings. Those children who survived infancy quickly took their places in the social and economic life of the family.[8]

Industrialization disrupted the unity of home and workplace, and as work was transformed into wage labor in factories and offices, the home took on a new meaning as haven from the pressures and pain of alienating work and school. The burden of domestic life and of creating a comfortable environment for others became women's work, work that was unpaid, devalued, and expected. In contrast to the economic value of women's labor in the past, a woman's devotion to home and family resulted in her economic dependence on her husband and psychological dependence on her children.[9]

The full-time mothering prescribed by this new ideology was appropriate only for a limited social class, namely the European and American middle class of the last two hundred years. Such a norm was not relevant for the majority of poor and working-class women. Racist ideology and social classification triumphed over sexist ideology for African–American and other ethnic and poor women as their roles as workers took precedence over motherhood. Since they were often expected to work long hours as domestic servants, these women had no choice but to leave the care of their own children to others.[10] More recently, women across race and class lines have moved full or part time into employment outside the home. Today, for the first time in American history, there are more women in the labor force than out of it,[11] working away from their children (if they have them).

Feminism and Maternalism

Yet despite past and present limited applicability, maternalism continues to shape contemporary thinking about women and to justify unequal social arrangements between women and men. This ideology has rarely faced organized challenge. What is often referred to as the "first wave" of the women's movement in the United States, which followed the rise of industrialization, extended the notion that women were inherently nurturant and morally superior to men. It was not until the early years of the "second wave" of feminism in the United States, during the late 1960s and into the mid 1970s, that there was a collective rebellion against the ideas that motherhood best defined women's place and that the cluster of associations surrounding the role best defined women's nature. Writers such as Betty Friedan, Shirley L. Radl, Jessie Bernard, and Adrienne Rich explored and destroyed idealizing myths that falsified the real experience of motherhood.[12] These women were among many European–American women who dared to speak about the exquisite maternal ambivalence they experienced.[13]

Feminists began to analyze motherhood as a social construction. The traditional ideology that posited biologically rooted essential differences between women and men was discredited as a strategy to maintain the subordination of women. Given the conditions of mothering imposed by a patriarchal and capitalist social order, the negative impact of motherhood on women's lives was explored and exposed.[14]

By the late 1970s, however, a new and competing strand of feminist thought gained currency. Mothering as a primarily positive characteristic of women reappeared in feminist thought. This shift occurred as women began to voice their strong desires to find fulfillment through mothering and caring for others and their pleasures in these activities. This maternal revivalism within contemporary feminism was seen by some as a response to aging among feminists and as a reaction to failures of public life for women.[15] For many women, the public space was a demoralizing place; motherhood, even with all its complexities, promised greater satisfactions.

The return to the view of mothering as valid and desirable work is a positive and critically important development within feminism and is in part a necessary corrective to single–focused indictments of motherhood's institutionalized aspects. The social role of mother provides women very positive opportunities for loving relationships and social contributions. Unfortunately, the return of motherhood within feminism has tended to provide new justification for the old ideology. The importance of motherhood and women's motherly qualities has reappeared in partnership with a critique of women's desires for autonomy and freedom—desires more often associated with not–mothers—as "male-like" and morally questionable, thus reinforcing traditional notions of gender.

The new and now dominant feminist scholarship on motherhood emphasizes a particularly female quality of caring and relatedness. Most feminists reject the notion that these personality characteristics are biologically determined. Rather, they are understood as being deeply rooted psychologically because of female mothering and as a result of the social practices of mothers. Aspects of traditional gender ideology have become the new common sense of feminism as conventional assumptions about masculinity and femininity are replicated and extended. This familiar but newly constructed view of woman has been seized with a vengeance[16] among feminists and has provided the basis for a new feminist "self-in-relation" psychology.[17]

Lynn Segal characterizes this new scholarship, which is found in writings across the disciplines, as "the mothering literature." Nancy Chodorow, Carol Gilligan, and Sara Ruddick[18] are among the key writers whose works comprise the mothering literature. Taken together, these theorists understand motherhood as the cause as well as the consequence of asymmetrical differences in needs, desires, fears, and talents between the gender groups.

In 1978, sociologist Nancy Chodorow published *The Reproduction of Mothering: Psychoanalysis and the Sociology of Gender.*[19] This often-cited and justly praised work provided a foundation for subsequent feminist theorizing about women's personalities. Chodorow's work was the most elaborate theoretical statement among the new writing on mothering and it was especially exciting and important to feminists.[20] Her work both reflected and reinforced the reassessment of motherhood beginning to take place. Feminists in the early 1970s had stressed the oppressive aspects of women's mothering, the conflicts, isolation, and economic dependence that most full-time mothers experienced, and the exhaustion of working mothers.[21] These analyses led to a central question: Given the cost of motherhood for women, why is it that most women continue to mother?

To answer the question of why women mother, Chodorow relied on the assumptions of the object-relations school of psychoanalysis. This school does not challenge the underlying premise on which Freud's work is based—that key elements of adult personality rest on early childhood experience.[22] However, Freud held that the successful resolution of the oedipal conflict resulted in satisfactory development. The British object-relations school, comprised of followers and critics of Freud, developed a theory that argued that crucial elements in a child's development originated much earlier than the oedipal period and from a different source than Freud believed. The preoedipal period, between birth and five years, was seen as critical to personality development. Rather than impulse control being of primary importance, the child's internalization or internal representation of important people and relationships (called "objects") became the focus for personality development. Chodorow summarized the development of personality according to object-relations theorists: personality is a result of a child's social relational experience from earliest infancy. These early relational experiences are internalized and organized by the child and come to constitute her or his personality.[23]

Using these psychoanalytic assumptions, Chodorow theorized two distinct and contrasting personality orientations for men and women. Since a *woman* is the caretaker for both sexes during infancy and early childhood, the interpersonal dynamics of gender identity formation differ for male and female children. The female's identity proceeds within a context of ongoing relationship as "mothers tend to experience their daughters as more like, and continuous with, themselves. Correspondingly, girls tend to remain part of the dyadic primary mother/child relationship itself. This means that a girl continues to experience herself as involved in issues of merging and separation, and in an attachment characterized by primary identification and the fusion of identification and object choice."[24]

Chodorow suggests that since the female child's feminine identity is continuous with her female mother she becomes "more open to and preoccupied with those relational issues that go into mothering."[25] Thus the desire to mother is reproduced from mother to daughter; mothers produce daughters with mothering capacities and needs.

The basic sense of self as connected to others is not a problem for women in and of itself. It is the capacity to separate self from other, to develop independent and autonomous identities, that becomes problematic for them. In contrast, men must sever their early identification with the female mother in order to establish a masculine identity. That identity is separate rather than relational; it remains fragile and it is implicated in the psychology of male dominance and the need to be superior to women. These contrasting personality orientations are fixed early in life. They are found globally since female mothering is universal and transhistorical.

The great importance of Chodorow's work is clear. Her analysis forms a base upon which other feminist-oriented psychologists and sociologists have theorized the importance of motherhood in the construction of gender. Drawing on Chodorow's work, the exploration of gender difference was carried forward and popularized by Carol Gilligan.[26] Her work stands at the forefront of the view that men and women have different, indeed in some ways opposite, orientations and perspectives toward nurturance, morality, and justice. Gilligan claims, for instance, that given early psychosocial experience, boys have selves "defined through separation," and girls have selves "delineated through connection."[27] Thus men as "selves-in-separation" find fulfillment as autonomous achievers, while women as "selves-in-connection" find fulfillment in their relationships with others. According to this schema, women tend to see danger in independence and achievement whereas men are threatened by intimacy and affiliation with others.

Gilligan further asserts that women feel a moral responsibility to discern and alleviate the troubles of the world whereas men's moral imperative appears as an injunction to respect the rights of others.[28] These moral differences are not biologically based but are psychologically produced. As sociologist Cynthia Fuchs Epstein points out, Gilligan's delineation of differences between men and women has been enthusiastically received by many feminist-oriented scholars who "regard her characterization of women's 'caring' morality as a positive orientation to behavior."[29] It is the cluster of associations surrounding motherhood—nurturing, caretaking, intimacy, and connections to others—which once again comes to define women.

The notion that women have distinctive virtues, connected to female mothering, gains power and legitimacy in the work of philosopher Sara Ruddick—this time with a twist. Ruddick devised the concept "maternal thinking."[30] Ruddick's thesis is that mothers develop a special perspective as a *result* of their experiences as nurturers of children. She identifies the following maternal virtues, here nicely summarized by philosopher Jean Grimshaw:[31]

> . . . *a responsiveness to growth* (and acceptance of change), along with a sort of learning that recognizes change, development, and the uniqueness of particular individuals and situations; *resilient good humour and cheerfulness,* even in the face of conflict, the fragility of life, and the dangers inherent in the processes of physical and mental growth; *attentive love,* which is responsive to the reality of the child, and is also prepared to give up, let grow, accept detachment; *humility,* a selfless respect for reality, a practical realism which involves understanding the child and respecting it as a person, without either "seizing" or "using" it.[32]

Through maternal work, mothers develop a protective concern for others, a healing rather than a harm-doing orientation, and cooperativeness, all qualities which provide a basis for pacifist commitment.[33] Men, as well as women, who are involved in maternal practices develop these distinctive ways of thinking and valuing. Although Ruddick's intent is to attend to the valuable outcomes of mothering work, which is highly appropriate, what are the implications of her ideas for not–mothers? By linking pro-social behavior so tightly to motherhood, she constructs women and men who do not engage in mothering as less responsive than parents to human well-being on an individual and social level. I will return to this point in later discussions.

In the analyses of the mothering theorists, then, motherhood directs women's lives in a continuous way. Motherhood is desired by women, since they are female mothered, and women's capacities to mother are further developed by their own mothering activities. Motherhood is both the source and the ultimate expression of women's capacities for care, relational identities, and superior values.[34] In short, the literature on gender polarizes men and women into two distinct and unified categories with motherhood as a central defining characteristic of woman.

Contemporary U.S. Culture and Maternalism

Maternalism persists, not only through academic discourses, but in institutional practices. For example, in the past decade medical interventions such as in vitro fertilization and embryo implants have expanded individual women's choices, but these technologies also reinforce "the master plan" for middle-class and wealthy women and reward those individuals who long for a child.[35] We live in an era where women and couples can catalog shop for sperm donors and where new techniques allow postmenopausal pregnancies. At the same time, decreased funding for the development of safe, effective, and affordable contraception and the continuing struggle over laws protecting the right to safe, legal, and funded abortions limit women's ability to avoid motherhood. Perhaps it is not surprising that these latter practices, which are inimical to patriarchal notions of woman's true vocation, are under attack.

Maternalist ideology is a central feature of consumer culture and functions as a backlash phenomenon, reasserting older gender roles against attempts to shift or transform power relations. Advertisers sell women's mothering along with designer diapers, orange juice, automobile tires, and airline companies. Supermothers stride forward, briefcase in one hand, child in the other, "managing to combine what 150 years of industrialization have split apart—child and job, frill and suit, female culture and male."[36] Such images suggest that women (not men) should and *can* happily "do it all," even though the rules of the culture have changed only moderately in the direction of gender justice. Such portrayals promote the essential connection between women and mothering. Regardless of their actual maternal status, all women are adversely affected by aspects of the resurgence of maternalism. Most real mothers fall short of the idealized supermother,[37] while childless women who cannot or who will not "have" children are judged defective or deviant. Piercing this ideology which links women's ultimate social and psychic fulfillment to mothering requires a direct challenge to the apparent inevitability of motherhood.[38]

The existence of women who intentionally remain childless contributes to such a challenge. This particular group of women contradicts dominant cultural expectations, all of which mandate women's mothering. Their stories also call into question feminist theorizing which privileges women's desire and capacity for motherhood over other interests and potentialities. In short, investigating the lives of women who do not fit society's notion of the average expectable woman, offers an opportunity to rethink both traditional and feminist promotions of universal womanhood. Since this group exists in conflict with prevailing constructions of gender and the institutional and social practices which such constructions maintain, their lives offer a rich source of insight.

The Current Contradictory Context

While the culture of motherhood is everywhere being rekindled, and remaining childless seems barely thinkable as an option, childlessness rates in the United States have gradually risen. These increasing rates reflect, in part, women's intentions. In June of 1988, fifteen percent of women forty to forty-four years old were childless,[39] well above the average childless rate of five to ten percent for most of this century. Demographer Amara Bachu finds that working women are more likely to decide to remain childless and that this phenomenon cuts across class lines.[40] Bachu does not find much difference between professional women choosing not to mother and those women employed in lower-paying service and factory jobs who make the same choice. The 1988 census figures also show that the desire to be childless crosses racial lines.[41]

Margaret Ambry, writing in *American Demographics* in April, 1992, projects "a stable but relatively high level of childlessness in the 1990's."[42] Urie Bronfenbrenner, a Cornell University professor, sees this trend as primarily adaptive. "We are the only modern nation that has no legal rights to maternity leave, let alone paternity leave. What else would you expect?"[43]

This slowly growing group of intentionally childless women exists unnoticed for the most part, except by demographers.[44] Childless women have received little attention from feminist theorists or in contemporary culture except for an occasional and often sensationalized article. This absence of attention to women who do not mother reinforces the notion that motherhood is *the* critical experience which both actualizes and symbolizes normality and maturity for women. Women who do not mother become aberrant at best, tragic at worst. Not–mothers' deviation from a statistical norm is stereotyped as misfortune or failure.

This historical moment, then, is indeed a contradictory one for women. Maternalism is in resurgence and more and more women are not assuming their "proper place." At the same time that women are being catapulted into the market economy in larger numbers than ever before in history, social policies and practices grounded in traditional gender ideology enforce and reinforce women's in-home responsibilities and out-of-home inequities. In such a climate, reproductive self-determination is severely constrained. In both directions, choices are in some sense forced. Women cannot make "free" choices to be mothers in an environment which encourages and enforces reproduction; neither can women "freely" choose to remain childless when the unrelieved pressures of parenthood fall on the shoulders of women without adequate supports. Simply said, maternalism interferes with the reproductive autonomy of women.

A Feminist Poststructural Approach

I bring to this study a political perspective on the world broadly defined as "feminist." Feminists recognize that women's individual lives are lived in a political context of oppression, accommodation, and resistance, that the personal and the political are thus intimately linked, and that social constructs have political purposes and are not simply neutral descriptors. Yet feminists disagree about causes and cures. The broad goal of feminist activity as I define it is the transformation of all relations of domination and subordination.[45] And I see the specific task of feminist scholars to be analysis of the workings of domination in all its manifestations—ideological, institutional, and subjective.[46] Feminists rely on various theories and approaches to accomplish this. The intent of this particular project, a study of a marginalized group of women which will not at the same time extend their marginalization, requires an approach which enables thinking about gender in terms of diversity rather than unity. A feminist poststructural orientation meets this requirement since conceptualizing, preserving, or rescuing difference is one of the central preoccupations of poststructuralists.[47]

Just as feminism is not monolithic but represents many different theoretical and practical strategies, what is called "poststructuralism" or "postmodernism" incorporates works that are very different from each other and often conflict. What I present here is an overview of key principles as articulated by philosopher Chris Weedon and political scientist and psychotherapist Jane Flax.[48]

Despite differences, all poststructuralist discourses are "deconstructive"; they seek to distance us from and make us skeptical about taken-for-granted ideas concerning truth, knowledge, power, self, and language that operate as legitimations for Western culture.[49] Deconstructivists are "masters of suspicion";[50] they seek to displace cherished meanings which then "open up spaces in or from which more varied ideas and practices may begin to emerge."[51] A primary contribution of a deconstructive strategy is the demystification (and thus weakening) of powerful ideologies.[52]

In short, a deconstructive strategy does not deny meaning, it *resists* what is given.

Such an approach makes deconstructivists disrespectful of authority, disruptive of all "natural" categories, and attentive to suppressed tensions within a text or story. There are political or ethical reasons for challenging universalizing theories or beliefs. For instance, in order to make "woman" appear as a unified category defined by fixed traits, discourses that contradict the apparent homogeneity must be erased, devalued, or suppressed. Any appearance of unity requires a prior act of violence, of forcibly suppressing certain elements in order to sustain that appearance of unity.

In contemporary Western societies, "the modern state and the 'human sciences' exist together in a complex, mutually interdependent network in which knowledge and power are inseparably intertwined."[53] As Flax explains:

> For example, Foucault argues the modern state must appeal to principles of reason and norms of "human nature" in order to have its laws considered legitimate and just. However, if human nature and reason are not inherently orderly and regular, the grounding of such laws would itself be unstable and constantly open to challenge by other interpretations and interpreters. The modern state thus depends on the creation and widespread acceptance of a fictive but persuasive account of "human nature" and on the emergence of a group of "experts" whose story about such questions will be considered authoritative and final.[54]

Those who do not act in accordance with "the laws of human nature" are defined as deviant. Deviations from the "normal" are dangerous to a political order founded on the regularities of human nature. Hence such behavior must be studied, regulated, and punished. The population is put under surveillance and is ideally trained to become self-governing by consciously or unconsciously accepting these laws of nature as principles guiding its own behavior.[55]

In summary, a feminist poststructuralist position claims that "social domination is based equally on material structures which create unequal material options for dominant and oppressed groups and on symbolic codes which regulate what is considered normal and deviant."[56] Domination is exercised through language and the manipulation of consciousness as well as through institutional practices and external force. Therefore, challenges to patriarchal social organization and to normative discourse are interconnected.

Language becomes an important site for political struggle. A key assumption for feminist poststructuralists is that it is language which enables us to think and speak and give meaning to the world. Language as a "meaning-constituting system,"[57] far from simply reflecting an already given social reality, actually *constructs* social reality. Language, in the form of conflicting "discourses," mediates between individuals and their real conditions of existence.[58]

Through the concept of discourse, "which is seen as a structuring principle of society, in social institutions, modes of thought and individual subjectivity,"[59] feminist poststructuralism is able to explain the workings of power on behalf of specific interests and to identify opportunities for resistance. Discourses exist in written and oral forms as well as in the social practices of everyday life. Power is exercised through language in the form of discourses.

Although there are always at any given time multiple ways to understand the world, not all versions of reality have equal social power. Hegemonic discourses or ideologies have strong institutional bases within the society. The plurality of experience ensures that powerful interest groups put a great deal of energy, time, and money into promoting certain views of the world.

Maintenance of patriarchal power requires discrediting or marginalizing ways of giving meaning to experience which re-define hegemonic gender norms.[60] For example, the notion that women who are not mothers are as normal as women who are threatens a central patriarchal norm. Diversity must be constructed as deviancy in order to maintain the association of womanhood with motherhood. Given this fact, the work of "normalizing" motherhood is carried on through the production and distribution of discourses that depreciate childless women. In this way the modern construction of deviance works to create hierarchies among women based on reproductive difference.

Woman as mother becomes central to the culture's symbolic order. "Mother" becomes the privileged term, appearing primary, complete. The second term, "not–mother," appears derived from the first, inferior, empty, and inescapably dependent upon it for its definition.[61] In this way, the definition of woman as mother appears universal. That which differs—the woman without children—is placed outside the definition of woman and becomes "other." In this way, positive definitions rest on the negation or repression of something presented as antithetical to it.[62]

The point here is that meaning is always relational, never intrinsic.[63] Motherhood, as the symbol of women's full self-realization, derives its power in relation to a negative counterpoint—childlessness. Severing the association of childlessness with deprivation and deficiency involves deconstructing the motherhood/childless opposition.

Feminist poststructuralism calls for the production and distribution of alternative constructions as well as for deconstructive writing. If much existing knowledge is understood to support women's subordinate social status by suppressing, distorting, and/or ignoring competing ways of giving meaning to experience,[64] then feminist scholarship becomes an "archeological endeavor,"[65] observing, describing, naming, and generating concepts that reconceptualize dominant understandings.

The feminist poststructuralism outlined above serves this study in three ways: as a source of central assumptions, as a set of tools for analysis, and as a guide for political practice. First, through this perspective I understand that remaining childless is not simply a personal act, but is rather a social practice which takes place in a highly politicized arena. Further, I believe that intentional not–mothers have a great deal to tell us about women's lives generally, about the power of hegemonic ideology, and about the human capacity for resistance. I also expect that remaining childless creates personal challenges for individual women which they must negotiate on a regular basis. The very existence of this group sustains pro-mothering ideology (by providing the negative image) and yet challenges that ideology (by providing a clear alternative). Thus I understand that not–mothering women are involved in conflicts over the meaning of reproduction and nonreproduction—conflicts which occur internally, interpersonally, and at the institutional level.

Secondly, this approach provides tools for analysis. Most importantly it directs research towards a study of the power of language in addition to the power of social institutions. It assists in the identification of key discourses which maintain the mother/not–mother hierarchical opposition and provides a method of challenge. While this book is not primarily a formal work of deconstruction, the approach appears at several key points below.

Finally, feminist poststructuralism provides a guide to political practice. One explicitly political goal of this practice is the "production, distribution, and transformation of meaning."[66] This goal recognizes that dominant discourses limit lives and serve interests. But it also recognizes that counter discourses, if made available, offer opportunities for change.

On Method

I decided to study childless women with a set of assumptions different from those of most researchers or writers on the subject.[67] Whether childlessness is assumed to be an abnormal or a healthy choice, the politics of reproductive difference remains hidden. By contrast, I view intentionally childless women as nonconformists who exist in a contradictory relationship to patriarchal ideology and capitalist social organization.

As Michelle Fine reminds us, women tell their stories in a culture committed to separating political awareness from personal experience. Thus women usually express their thoughts and feelings in personal terms, and do not tie them to social relations and conditions.[68] I see it as my work to bring politics to their words, to politically interpret their voices. I understand the complexity and risk of this intervention, and make every effort to "achieve the best approximations of 'reality'"[69] as I expose women's voices. But I do not shrink from what I view as an essential and indeed unavoidable task of interpretation.

My research is based on intensive interviews with thirty-four married, intentionally childless women ranging in age from forty to seventy-eight. Four of the women were in long-term, live-in heterosexual relationships ("common-law" marriages), and the rest were legally married. I limited the sample to married women since the social pressure to mother is greatest within this context. I interviewed women in their forties and older since I wanted a sample of *permanently* childless women. I made sure that the younger women in the sample, who were not quite past childbearing years, were deeply committed to their nonreproductive status. Participants were recruited nationwide through a strategy which combined network sampling and advertising through professional newsletters and women's periodicals, with outreach to community groups serving middle-aged and later life women. I conducted, taped, and transcribed eight telephone interviews and twenty-six in-person interviews, all lasting at least two hours. My final sample included three women in their seventies, one in her sixties, two in their fifties, nineteen between the ages of forty-five and forty-nine, and the remaining nine in their early forties.

With a planned small sample size, I had to keep the population relatively homogenous. All participants were European–American with one exception, a Latina. All participants were able-bodied with one exception, a woman who had a congenital spinal disability. Women's ethnic backgrounds turned out to be an important source of identification. A significant number of participants were from first or second generation immigrant families, mostly from Eastern Europe. Nine women were Jewish, eleven women had been raised Catholic, and fourteen had been raised in various Protestant traditions.

Women worked as academics, school teachers, psychologists, social workers, artists, administrators. Some were full-time students or retired. Two physicians, a lawyer, a stockbroker, an architect, a store owner, a librarian, a nutritionist, a corporate executive, and a film producer were among the group. All but one woman had at least a college education. The majority had advanced educational degrees.

Given financial and population constraints, I could not produce an "unbiased" sample. The conclusions I reach in my research are bounded by the limits of the sample. Yet my belief is that the value of this project is not dependent on its generalizability but rather on its conceptual creativity and convincing criticism.

The Issues of Class and Race

When the subject of intentionally childless women appears, the assumption is nearly always made that this "choice" is the province of middle- and upper middle-class women. Researchers support this assumption by looking at present class status only. An unexpected finding of my research was that a full three-quarters of the women identified themselves as coming from either poor or working-class backgrounds. And they often connected their upward class mobility directly to the decision to remain childless. This statistic lends support to writer Carolyn Kay Steedman who, reflecting on her own working-class childhood, asserts that it is to the marginal and secret stories of working-class women that we must look for a "disturbance of that huge and bland assumption that the wish for a child largely structures femininity."[70]

Researchers and members of the majority culture commonly assume that intentional childlessness is the exclusive domain of white women. A 1989 study by Robert Boyd reviews black and white childlessness differences over the past century, and reports that approximately one-third of African–American women in the birth cohort 1900–1919 were permanently childless, exceeding the childless rate of white women. This is a significant statistic. Boyd challenges what he sees as "racist assumptions" of interpreters of this figure who link it to the poor health of black women. Rather,

Boyd contends that this high rate reflects, in part, individual intention and the desire for class mobility.

The assumption that childless women are primarily white is related to the fact that most *studies* of such women are conducted by and are about European–Americans. Indeed this book fits that characterization. But as Boyd's research makes clear, many women of color do remain childless, and they have their stories to tell. Institutional racism, differing relations to "nuclear" families, and class location are all part of those stories, and their words contribute in essential ways to reconceptualization of motherhood and childlessness.

Two recent anthologies include the voices of racial and ethnic women. In *Childlessness Transformed,* Brooke Medicine Eagle tells of the difficulties facing Crow Indian women trying to mother on—and off—the reservation, and of her own experiences as an intentionally childless woman.[71] *Childless By Choice: A Feminist Anthology* includes writings by women of diverse backgrounds and ages, including Chicana, African–American, Native American, lesbian, urban, and rural women.[72] Another recent book, *Women Without Children,* includes women from various backgrounds and situations, including African–American women and lesbian women, although not all identify as intentionally childless. And in a 1990 issue of *Essence,* forty-three year old African–American Jennifer Jordan discloses her fears about mothering and her contentment with aunthood.[73]

The experiences of women of color who resist motherhood need to be further documented and explored. This is not my project. However, if the women in my sample are not statistical reflections of all childless women, their stories do speak to issues likely to be important to all women who are or consider being intentionally childless. Maternalist ideology, discourses of deficiency and regret, conflicts with friends, concerns about a future without the social support of children, are important to all childless women because they are childless. While there are significant differences among not–mothering women, there are meaningful commonalities as well.

Naming Women Who Choose Not to Mother

Words not only name objects, they convey attitudes. A variety of terms are used to describe women I studied: "childless," "child-free," "non–mother." Each term is politically and analytically problematic. "Childless" and "non–mother" not only tell us a woman is not a mother; they tell us that a void exists.[74] Each word reinforces the mother standard, emphasizes absence—something is missing. The defining characteristic is a lack, with an implication that the persons so identified are less than those without the lack. The term "non-white" comes to mind as a comparable word.

"Child-free" is a word some feminists use who wish to contradict patriarchal meaning. Yet for me, this term has a presumptuous ring to it. It suggests that women who do not have children of their own want to be rid of children, as in those who promote a "union-free" or "smoke-free" environment. The notion that not–mothers may be hostile to children does not offer an accurate or politically useful countercultural construction. Each term reinforces the dominant ideology which views mother as superior.

My preference would be for the creation of a new word, as we use the term "single" (not marriedless or marriage–free) or "lesbian" (not manless or male–free). But the creation of new terms is difficult and often causes confusion among readers. For these reasons I adopt the terms childless and not–mother, but with the recognition of the political risks of such a choice. Not–mother seems more descriptive and less encompassing than non–mother. The words of women who are not mothers, recorded in the chapters ahead, will make clear that their lives are not simply the vacant opposite of motherhood.

One final note on language. Following the lead of Elizabeth Kennedy and Madeline Davis,[75] I call the women I interviewed "narrators," since the interview was, in part, an oral history approach. For variety, I also use the term "participant." I prefer these two designations to the rather distant social scientific denotations "respondent" or "subject."

In the Chapters Ahead

In the chapters ahead, I document the personal challenges facing individual not–mothers, and I use their experiences and
interpretations to illuminate the ways that maternalism is main-
tained and enforced through routine social practices and through
discourses on childlessness. I use my analyses to question and
expand existing feminist theories of gender.

In "Troubling Developments," I examine the oral histories of
narrators and I identify patterns which interfere with the reproduction of mothering. I use the knowledge gained to unsettle popular
notions about women's nature and development. In "Explaining
the Choice," I analyze the stories women tell to account for their
childlessness. Women did not find it easy to put their experiences
into words but could not escape the "explanatory work" demanded by others. Their efforts to give answers were complicated by the
language of "choice," a confounding interpretative framework.

The next two chapters deal with symbolic distinctions between
mothers and childless women. In the dominant culture, motherhood is idealized while childlessness is seen as an affliction. Three
specific discourses constructing not–mothers, "derogation," "compensation," and "regret," dichotomize women into loving, fulfilled
mothers versus selfish, emotionally empty women. Maternalist ideology, I argue, depends on the depreciation of not–mothering
women in order to influence women's behaviors in the direction of
motherhood. Some women found it necessary to come to terms
with internalized negative beliefs. Narrators, aware of symbolic
censure, reconstructed customary meanings.

In "The Social World of Childless Women," I focus on women's
affiliations with partners, children, and friends—especially mothers.
I describe the power and vulnerability that come from living in a
"couple nest," and I recount the solidarity and distances that characterize relationships with children. I also discuss the "friendship
wedges" women describe in their associations with other women
who are mothers. I relate these tensions to the differing penalties
and privileges accorded to contrasting reproductive preferences.

The most important privilege of childless living that women consistently identify is "freedom!" Yet as I explore in the final section of this chapter, such freedom is not without contradictions.

In the concluding chapter, I summarize the ways that remaining childless creates personal trials for individual women, and the ways that this group challenges existing ideas about women. Drawing on various feminist writings and my own ruminations, I briefly muse about ways we might move into more expansive and humane ways of living together as a human community. My hope is that these reflections will invite more scholarly work and social action aimed at promoting reproductive diversity.

2

"I think of myself as a product of the times"
TROUBLING DEVELOPMENTS

Wanting a baby, it's never been a part of me. It's like I have some homosexuals in my clientele and they always remember being attracted to someone of the same sex. You know, it just was a part of their life. And I think that's the way it was for me. There was never a conflict.

—Elizabeth, age 48

If female identity is an irreducible core, then what role can be given to society, history, and language in shaping the subject position of women? In place of these cultural forces stands a lone figure, the mother.

—Janice Doane & Devon Hodges[1]

FEMINISTS stir up trouble.[2] According to Judith Butler, feminism's mission is to trouble gender categories that have been made to seem natural, including those constructions of femininity and masculinity most favored by feminists at any given point in time.[3] This chapter employs key stories told by not–mothering women to paint a more contradictory picture of women's identities and development than is currently fashionable.

Much recent work on gender and women's development assumes or documents the reproduction of mothering. Psychoanalytic and sociological accounts describe the forces that shape women's identities early in life to conform to a central cultural mandate of femininity. For the most part, this literature suggests that women participate in relatively homogeneous and predictable intrapsychic and social processes leading to the desire and capacity for mother-hood. Little attention is given either to contradictions in these processes or to women's resistances to conformity. Relational dis-course has replaced the liberation discourse of the 1970s.

Study of the oral histories of women who define themselves as intentionally childless does not provide a unified and comprehensive developmental theory of its own. It does call into question universalizing tendencies within existing theories, and it provides an opportunity for reflection on patterns which may interfere with predictable conformity to dominant norms, including but not lim-ited to motherhood.

I do not assume that women who define themselves as inten-tionally childless are *essentially* different from women who are mothers. I do believe, given their reproductive status and resultant social location, not–mothering women may act on, emphasize, and develop potentialities that exist in all women—potentialities that are often denied or discouraged. Since narrators were being inter-viewed because they had violated a major norm, perhaps they comfortably stressed aspects of their experience that didn't fit gen-der expectations. Although I articulate patterns where I see them, there is enormous intragroup variation among women who do not have children. In the discussion below, I try to attend to the differ-ences as well as the commonalities that exist among childless women.

In the following pages, after I describe my method of soliciting oral histories and discuss some general patterns found in the writ-ten outlines I collected, I present and analyze the oppositional knowledge embedded in those histories. The stories women tell about themselves allow for the grand variations in talents and ori-entations that actually exist among—and within—women.

Whose Life Course Is It, Anyway?

In order to get a sense of how women in my sample constructed their lives and built identities across a changing life course, I asked each participant to complete a brief written autobiographical exercise before our interview. An adaptation of an Intensive Journal exercise was used which instructed women to think about their lives as a book and to name eight or ten periods or "chapters."[4] The intent of the written exercise was two-fold. First, I did not wish to assume which events or changes in the women's lives were significant for them and which were not. I wanted them to construct their stories on their own terms. Second, I wanted each participant to talk about her past, present, and future so I could view her reproductive decision within the context of her own developing life.

I expected that some prior thinking by narrators would facilitate our work together. During the interview I asked participants to describe each period in more detail and I integrated questions from my interview schedule at the appropriate times. For instance, when a woman spoke of her childhood, I would ask questions about her parents' occupations and how she perceived her class background if she herself did not provide this information.

The "book" outlines women constructed varied in form and content; some constructions were straightforward and descriptive, others symbolic and valuative. Some women wrote one word "chapters" while others wrote paragraphs about each period they identified. Most, however, recorded a single phrase that represented the transition points in their lives as they felt or understood them. Participants' chapters rarely outlined dramas of family life or emphasized relationships. Indeed, neither family nor relationships figured prominently in their writings. One woman, a psychologist, shared with me the fact that the exercise was a powerful and surprising experience for her. I asked her to explain:

> What I put down and what I omitted was what was surprising to me . . . It makes sense knowing my life, but family I'm not really including. I talk about a relationship later, that's with my husband. But the family stuff . . . I know what various people I know would have put, the family would have been threaded all through the stages, and there's no hint of it anywhere in mine, really.
>
> Elizabeth, age 48

Another woman, older than most of the narrators, spoke of the insight she had from writing an autobiographical outline:

> Now, doing that (exercise) gave me a little insight into myself. I knew but I didn't know. I went putting the chapters down and I'm glad Ronald isn't here at this moment, this might be bad for his ego. Most of it is in reference to me and my work and *not* marriage. You have guaranteed anonymity, so, I'd hate to say this in front of Ronald. But I realized—the first time really—that if I could have just one of the two things, looking back, the career, I can't *imagine* my life without the career. I *can* imagine my life without marriage.
>
> Anonymous

One third of the women who, in fact, are married did not mention marriage as a significant event:

> I noticed that I didn't even write down marriage as being a separate episode. I think it's because it was just part of being a grad student with Frank. So marriage doesn't sort of stand out which is funny.
>
> Isabel, age 45

> You know, it was a funny thing. Chapters in my life. I went through nine of them and I said, "Do you know, I haven't said one thing about me apart from certain achievements, or certain school periods in my life, like college or graduate school or whatever, or my job." So I kind of lumped in under ten my affective life, you know, that I'm married.
>
> Cathy, age 45

This is not to say that their marriages are unimportant. To the contrary, the majority of women went on to describe deep and loving relationships, as I will discuss later. One woman, upon noticing she had left marriage off the outline of her life, stated she could not imagine life without her husband but she thought about their relationship as "the backdrop" of her adult story. However, as critical as these relationships are to most of the women, they are not at the center of the narratives they invented.

Chapters were most often constructed around geographical location, historical events, educational and work transitions. As one woman said about her outline, "Well, I think it's chronological and most of the chapters I did by vocation. I found that was the easiest. Well, I guess I did it by school and vocation. I have two different ways to recall." A strong generational consciousness was in evidence as women more often wrapped stories around historical circumstances than around life stages.

Regardless of how women organized their autobiographies, as they talked their outlines became animated stories of their efforts to forge their own paths and to actualize potentials against various odds. Their own development was at center stage, although their histories in no way implied not needing or caring for and about others. Women spoke fluently about the emotional and instrumental support they received from family members, friends, mentors, and so on. Women spoke as well of the inspiration and courage they got from other women's written words. It was not uncommon for participants to name a specific book or books that fueled nonconventional behaviors.[5]

Most often, women understood their adult growth proceeding primarily through participation in educational institutions and through work experiences. For numerous women who described their backgrounds as working-class, attending college was perceived as perhaps the key event in the life history. As Susan, age 74, said it: "When I was twenty-two I began going to college at night. And this opened a new world for me. I came to life. It made such a difference. It was just unbelievable. It opened a different world." Regardless of class background, more women than not spoke of strong commitments to work and of their initial hesitancies as adults to enter into committed relationships which might jeopardize their purposeful identities. Women commonly negotiated work-centered lives before entering into marriages.

The "work" that women built identities around was not necessarily a career or even paid employment. For instance, one woman defined herself as "a professional feminist, and that gets manifested as a therapist and as an educator, and in the past my professional feminism has been as a performer." Another woman saw her interest in history and "the whole thread of activism" as central to her sense of self. Others who were not professionally or career-oriented, took "jobs" in order to remain economically independent while pursuing their "real work" as animal advocates, community activists, or participants in cultural activities. For a small minority, the notion of "important work" was unimportant; rather, they described themselves as vitalists or adventurers, simply wanting to enjoy life and diverse experiences.

Related to the fact that narrators did not follow the "expected" life course, women reported feeling chronologically out-of-sync. Rather than being in tune with their own age cohort, women reported having younger and older friends—those who did not yet have children and those whose children were grown. As Donna, age 43, told it: "I really lost touch with people my own age because people my own age were home with babies." In several cases, chronological discontinuity was related to or exacerbated by a significant age difference between marital partners. When Donna married a man fourteen years her senior, she entered a network of people older than herself. In another case, a participant was twenty-eight years younger than her husband. And in two cases, interviewed women were fourteen years older than their spouses.

Women consistently reported feeling younger than their biological age. Several women related this directly to childlessness and not having to "settle down." For example, Louise, who put off a committed relationship until she turned thirty, was a world-wide traveler in her twenties. During her thirties, she and her husband were both graduate students and "heavy duty activists." At age forty-three she feels she "is doing what other people did in their twenties, you know, saving money, buying a house, staying with one job for more than a year and a half, being bourgeois in some ways but not real bothered about it at this point."

Elaine described having a sense of herself as a mature and highly responsible person, yet feeling somehow "not grown up." She related this feeling to not having to take "the mother–stance" and assume a certain knowledge and give authoritative advice:

> There might be something about being childless that you're not tied to age stages—you're not assuming those roles of having to help people

grow up—so you don't have to stand there and say, "I'm grown up and I'm going to help you grow up . . ."

Elaine, age 48

Later in the interview, Elaine speculated that "being childless keeps you from realizing how old you are." Working and identifying with students and colleagues younger than herself, she feels "disoriented" about how old she is. And she wonders if her strong identification with work, "which is ageless in a sense," plays a role in this disorientation. She wonders if mothers, as they watch their children grow, are reminded of their own age in a way that she is not. Whatever the reasons, feeling a "chronological weirdness," as one woman put it, was part of the experience that not–mothers reported as they reviewed their lives.

In *Interpreting Women's Lives,* The Personal Narratives Group makes the point that the stories women tell are rarely told without reference to the dynamics of gender.[6] "Women's personal narratives are, among other things, stories of how women negotiate their 'exceptional' gender status both in their daily lives and over the course of a lifetime."[7] The life stories I collected as women discussed their book outlines may be considered "counter-narratives, since they reveal that the narrators do not act, think or feel the way they are 'supposed to.'"[8] As such, the stories reproduced below can serve to "expose the viewpoint embedded in dominant ideology as particularist rather than universal . . ."[9]

Unwomanly Conduct

In the following pages I experiment with answers to two questions: First, what early forces do participants describe as impacting on gender conformity? And second, how does this knowledge disturb taken-for-granted notions about women's nature and development more generally?

The investigation suggests four forces which contradict the reproduction of mothering: women's subversive desires for independence, for adventure, for self-defined development; the economic circumstances of women's childhoods and the longings for improvement which arise out of their situations; social conditions of the times; and experiences of exclusion which, along with nontraditional interests, lead to the development of positively-valued nonconformist identities.

Subversive Desires

With the written exercise as a guide, a portion of each of my interviews was devoted to listening to the participant's oral history. Each interview included considerable material on childhood and early adulthood. While the early stories women told were by definition unique, many shared a common plot of wanting more and different experiences than traditionally allowed. In order to venture out and pursue their own interests and talents, the women necessarily resisted and transgressed limitations imposed by gender norms. Direct defiance was often demanded; in cases where expectations were not so fixed and rigid, rebellion was not required, but at least acting "strange" or "different" was.

Compelling desires for self-expansion, for an education, for economic self-sufficiency, were realized through some combination of confrontation, negotiation, and determination.[10] Their struggles to create lives to their liking provide insights into the ways women's development is shaped, constrained, and disciplined in this culture. Their stories demonstrate that women's development does not just "proceed" in some orderly fashion. Women must constantly engage in acts of subversion if they pursue goals that are not stereotypically feminine ones.

The tales begin with the women describing their very early wishes for a full range of activities and their resistances to the constraints of "femininity." Without interviewer prompting, several women told doll stories which are particularly illustrative:[11]

> My mother always bought me dolls. I didn't like dolls. I didn't want dolls. I wanted puzzles. I wanted airplanes. I wanted trains, which are not things that little girls play with. I was told to play with dolls. You

are supposed to dress them, comb their hair, but you couldn't get a comb through it. It was very frustrating. I got to the point that I really got quite angry about it. I remember taking one doll down the basement and cracking its head on the cement wall thinking, "maybe that will teach her, I DON'T LIKE THESE THINGS!"

Doris, age 49

As a child I liked boy's toys. I remember walking past a store window with my father and seeing this beautiful red fire engine and I wanted it. I *really* wanted it. We went into the store and my father bought me a doll. When we got home I *threw* the doll across the room and it smashed. I remember my father being surprised.

Carole, age 55

I hated dolls. Every Christmas the same thing would happen to me. My mother would hopefully buy me dolls and clothes and things like that and my mother reminds me of it. I still remember hiding sometimes when I would see her coming with her dolls . . . I did a lot of reading. I just didn't get my jollies from dressing dolls.

Linda, age 40

Not all doll stories involved such dramatic resistance. While not rejecting dolls, another woman simply remembers having other interests which took precedence. Jane spoke of being influenced by cowboys on television. She remembers dressing up in her cowboy outfit year after year, riding a broomstick, her horse:

I had dolls but I was never really interested in them. I never really asked for them. I asked for horses . . . I had guns—not that I was interested in shooting people. It was part of the outfit. I was more interested in the ability to get on your horse and ride away far and ride away fast and stuff like that. The freedom and the power that you feel.

Jane, age 41

My intent here is not to use these narratives to reify not–mothering women into a separate category absolutely distinct from mother. My guess is that many mothers did not have dolls at the center of their play. And some of the women I interviewed also reported acting like little mothers. (One woman washed worms in her dollhouse bathtub, assuming the creatures did not want to be dirty. Most likely, young girls show interest in activities that span the labels masculine and feminine.) My point in sharing these stories is to demonstrate how gender norms organize the daily lives of children in an immediate way, and, for girls may channel energy into caretaking activities. Parents, motivated to do what they believe is in the best interests of their daughters, act on common-sense assumptions about the differences between women and men. "Everybody knows that little girls want dolls." The power of such knowledge comes from its claim to be natural and therefore true. Yet such knowledge is hardly true or fixed, as demonstrated by these women's stories. It represents specific patriarchal values and interests.[12] The gendering process is inconsistent and partial, as these daughters demonstrate. Hardly simple victims of gender ideology, when there is no correspondence between their personal proclivities and gender-defined interests, they become ornery.

Beyond their experiences with pro-mothering social practices, women told stories about attempts to discipline their bodies, movements, clothing, and even color preferences. One woman, whose first chapter of her life/book was titled "Pink Was My Least Favorite Color," had this to say:

> I think I was struck by that title because when I was in school many years ago I remember writing a paper with this title. It reflects the fact that there were expectations of me as a very young child that I remember being unwilling to meet that had to do with being a girl. And keeping oneself perfectly prim and perfectly clean all day and sitting and doing some passive form of entertainment or exercise for myself. And feedback from my mother that it was difficult to put me into a dress in the morning and know that in two or three hours it would be ruined in some way, shape or form. And I remember disliking pink intensely. Relatives and friends buying me things in pink and me refusing to wear them.
>
> Sara, age 46

Here again commonsense knowledge plays a key role in maintaining the centrality of gender difference as a locus of power in society.[13] The social expectations that girls should be caretakers and look pretty and act "ladylike" while boys should assert themselves forcefully in the social world are related to boys' and girls' future social destinations within a patriarchal society. Dominant norms are constantly reaffirmed as part of the commonsense knowledge upon which individuals draw for understanding and guidance.[14] In such a context, as the above stories demonstrate, self-development for women becomes a political activity, involving resistance to imposed norms and transgression of set boundaries. In short, self-development is an emancipatory project.

Other vignettes of resistance, rebellion, and defiance are found in abundance in the autobiographies of the women I interviewed. An attitude of "says who?" was described again and again. Women told of early dissatisfactions with "appropriate" gender assignments and of wanting something different for themselves at a time when they did not yet have a clear sense of what alternatives existed. They knew what they *didn't* want even if they weren't sure what they *did* want:[15]

> At first, in my teens, in my dating, in talking to young people, I felt very much out of things. Because then I still had no role model. And I was striving for something and I didn't quite know what. But I knew it wasn't going to be what was *there*. It wasn't going to be *that*. I didn't want *that*.
>
> Susan, age 74

> What was assumed was that I would go to college but it was also pretty much assumed that I would go to [the local Catholic college] and become a teacher or a nurse. And I just said, "NO." What was really interesting is that I literally did not know what the other choices were . . . I just became determined that I wasn't going to do that.
>
> Donna, age 45

Mothers, of course, were implicated in the imposition of gender norms. But in many instances, participant's nontraditional interests were not only tolerated, but received maternal support. As women told it, such support was related to their mothers' own experience with and resentment of gender-based constraints:

> I remember—now these are some important things. I remember stories that my mother used to tell me. She'd say, "I'm going to be very

sure that nobody ever stops you from being what you want to be." I mean, she said this in reference to the fact that her father wouldn't let her be what she wanted to be. And also, she always wanted to work outside the home. And I didn't realize this until I was quite a bit older, until I was in college even, and Daddy did not want her working outside the home. In fact, she never learned to drive. And so she even went so far as to tell me, you know, "I will see to it that your Daddy doesn't keep you from being what you want to be if you know what you want to do."

Augusta, age 48

In this situation, Augusta's mother aligns herself with her daughter's interests against the father's power to confine and control.

The class aspirations of both parents played into providing support for their daughter's nonconventional pursuits as well, as long as such pursuits were related to increasing social power. One woman, identified with her Latina heritage, spoke of the great gender-based restrictions that she was subject to, greater in intensity than those in the Anglo world.[16] In Gloria's culture, at age seventeen she was considered, in her words, "an old maid." In her teens she experienced great pressure to drop out of high school, get married, and have children. And at this point her mother came to her defense:

My mother, God love her, finally started saying things, "leave Gloria alone, Gloria is different." I think she started saying that when I was about fifteen because I remember getting pressure about "why do you have to go to high school, nobody else goes to high school. You get married and have kids." And my mother would say, "well yes, but Gloria does it a little different, she's always done it a little different ever since she was this high, so leave her alone."

Gloria, age 43

Her father also provided instrumental support to her early desires for an education and to become a teacher. He would spend his Saturdays taking her to the library where he would wait outside while she read. This is a moving portrait of a father's devotion to his daughter's development which contradicted some of his own beliefs about women's appropriate role. These parents' support of their daughter's ambitions illustrates the way class and gender norms can clash in the lives of women and within their families of origin.

The role of the mother in her daughter's development often emphasizes the negative. Mothers are seen as conservative influences, socializing daughters into patriarchal roles, beliefs, and behaviors, in essence, as the mediators of patriarchy. While this is partially accurate, lack of attention to the ways mothers support their daughters' bids for freedom obscures contradictions in development. Women in this study commonly depicted their mothers as allies, often against fathers, in their search for "something different." Participants resisted aspects of the gendering process given their own dispositions; they also learned from their mother's resistances and ambivalence.

An Aside on "Unhappy Childhood Experiences"

The preceding section focuses on positive parental support for difference. Of course not all childhood stories were so happy. Several women described experiences in dysfunctional families and some had stories to tell of parental inadequacies. However, respondents did not tie their resistance to gender norms to these experiences alone. Familial support seemed as important to them as family problems in their self-development.

The literature on childless women gives considerable attention to women's negative family experiences,[17] but there is little evidence from my sample that women without children are more likely to have such experiences than women with children. Indeed, many women may *have* children in the hope that they will be able to create a better family experience than they had as children.

One woman in my sample had a clear answer to the equation of unhappy childhood with childlessness. A therapist once linked her desire to remain childless to an unhappy childhood. She responded:

> Well, if that's the case the world should have stopped reproducing centuries ago . . . if that (a happy childhood) was the criterion for having a child then we wouldn't be here having this conversation.
>
> Sara, age 46

Participant's stories demonstrate that the linking of childlessness to unhappy childhoods is simplistic. But worse, it is also oppressive, because it assumes only negative sources for women's choices to be different. Thus difference is associated with unhappiness and conformity with happiness. As a later chapter will demonstrate, when such ideas filter into the popular culture, they can create stress for women who intentionally remain childless.

Class Aspirations

The third chapter I wrote down says: "Who says that's all there is?" When Peggy Lee made that song years ago I felt as if she had read my mind.

Sara, age 46

Many women's early desires for a life different from that traditionally allowed are related not only to their personal interests as discussed above but to their parents' and their own class aspirations. As noted earlier, an unexpected finding of this study, one that contradicts common assumptions about who chooses childlessness, is that nearly three-fourths of the participants describe themselves as coming from poor or working-class backgrounds. Although class is notoriously hard to measure, women most often linked the class assignment to a combination of educational attainment and economic conditions. Augusta spoke of her "Daddy's third grade education," Jane spoke of her mother working in a factory to support her three children, Maria spoke of her father being "blue collar," a mechanic in a factory for most of his working life. Mary's father drove a truck and worked as a laborer. Gloria spoke of her parents living in poverty.

In the stories they constructed, "wanting more and different" is linked to desires for class mobility.[18] Those women who identified themselves as having middle-class to upper middle-class origins also received support to achieve outside the restricted "feminine" sphere. This is related to class, but in a different fashion. Academic achievement was "expected." Parents wanted their daughters to excel in school. Yet such expectations were often associated with proper preparation for marriage and motherhood, and with making a "good marriage," i.e. marrying within or above class of origin. Such a scenario was not seen as jeopardizing class standing. Women from working-class backgrounds did not grow up with the same expectation that they could count on marriage to provide ongoing economic well-being. The desire to transcend class of origin and the limitations associated with it required rebellion from the mandates of gender, as Gloria succinctly states:

> If I had been nice and complacent and pleasing I would probably be living in Florida, with six kids. Probably a high school dropout, married to a mechanic and probably not doing very well economically, probably wondering how I'm going to pay my next bill. Not that there is anything wrong with that, if that's what you choose to do. But that's not what I chose to do. So maybe my rebelliousness and my headstrongness is related to why I am a doctor.
>
> Gloria, age 43

The gender/class conflict is again described by the daughter of second generation immigrants:

> My father has said a few times that he wishes I lived down the block and had kids, but I think they in many ways created a monster, from their values and their point of view. They pushed the self-reliance and they pushed the pursuit of an education and they pushed me to go into a career without having any foresight as to what that meant.
>
> Linda, age 40

In Linda's case, the necessity to insure an economically self-sufficient life because "men die, men leave, lots of things happen to men and you cannot be totally dependent on a man . . . was a theme that was pounded into me." The contradictory pressures experienced by this university professor and successful free-lance consultant were resolved as class aspirations overrode gender expectations.

Many women described the support they received from parents as directly related to class issues. When Elizabeth described her family as "working-class," I asked her why she assigned them this status. Her father worked on a railroad and her mother had not graduated from high school. Along with not having much money and living in a "modest" place, she identified her parents' "desire for their child to achieve because she could do better than they had," as a "working-class" value. Augusta described her parents, who had not progressed very far in school, as wanting to be sure she went to college "because you never know when you will need to support yourself." Such constructions suggest that these women received mixed messages from their parents, at once encouraging and discouraging "normal" gender identification.[19]

My findings echo those of Barbara Levy Simon who, when studying the lives of never–married women, found that the African–American women in her sample grew up with a stronger imperative to get out of poverty than to marry.[20] To quote Simon, "Most were encouraged to marry, but not with the urgency with which they were exhorted to 'get an education,' a good job, and to stay close to God."[21] Similarly, Carolyn Kay Steedman, reflecting upon her own working-class childhood, links the ambivalence about motherhood that her mother experienced to her longings for the material and social benefits of class power.[22] She connects her mother's class aspirations to the continuous warning she received: "'Never have children dear; they ruin your life.'"[23]

Not all narrators' parents encouraged class mobility. Frustrated by her parents' acceptance of their social location and concomitant lack of money, education, and "culture," a woman born to Eastern–European Jewish parents describes her frustration:

I grew up in South Philadelphia which was a ghetto-like experience years and years ago. And I had the belief that there had to be more than I could see and hear going on around me . . . It wasn't uncommon for me, even at eight or nine or ten, to take my fifteen cents and literally disappear for the day and take a trolley car into center city and then walk to Rittenhouse Square and take the bus and go to the University of Pennsylvania library to just *look* and listen. And I continued to do that for ten years until I was about seventeen. Going into neighborhoods where people were more prominent, where people were more educated, where there was a lot more abundance than

what I had access to. And being terribly curious about how it was that
they got there . . . So my curiosity just continued to take me out into
the world to find out what other lifestyles were possible and what
other dreams could be attained.

Sara, age 46

Sara spoke of relationships with men as hazardous to accomplish-
ing "the ten-year plan" she devised for herself in her early twenties.
Her agenda included completing school, establishing a professional
career, living abroad, and writing. Her decision to stay out of a relationship was not experienced as a deprivation but as "entering a
whole new reality . . . What for me was more exciting is that I had a
ten-year plan and a lot of outcomes to achieve in that ten-year period and they were all going to come true. I didn't know how,
exactly, but they were all going to happen. And they did."

Donna, now a successful lawyer, spoke of her growing awareness
of wanting more education, nicer "material things," and more
"cultural experiences" than her parents had. "Something said that
there had to be more. Maybe it was the babysitting experience that
got me into a lot of different homes where I could see how other
people were living." For Donna, as for many others I interviewed,
getting an education was perceived as the best strategy to assure
higher class standing without having to depend on and/or subordinate oneself to a man, which was perceived as a risky proposition.
Lee, now in her sixties, told of her own motivation to "break
ground" and be the first in her immigrant family to attend college.
"I wanted an education and that sort of thing rather than anything
else." Her desire was fueled by her mother's belief before her that
"there is *nothing* more important than an education."[24]

These self-portraits raise questions about the notion of a stable
and monolithic feminine orientation. These women did marry but
usually not at the expense of self-defined agendas. The stories suggest a flaw in the current tendency to privilege women's relational
needs and capacities above coexisting desires for social power and
achievement.

The stories told above hardly fit the 1990s notions of what
women want and need. However, they do fit the post-Depression

decades of the 1960s and 1970s when historical forces gave rise to various liberation movements. The preoccupation with independence that dominates the stories of participants can be related not only to personal proclivities and class aspirations but to "cohort effects" which played a major role in shaping their desires and behaviors.

Historical Forces

In contradiction to the universalizing theory that women need and desire motherhood because of early psychosocial experiences, the life stories that intentionally childless women tell point up historical variations in the importance and desirability of motherhood. The *meanings* of motherhood change as economic and social conditions change. With the rise of object-relations psychoanalysis in the last part of the twentieth century, the bond between mother and child has taken on a near-sacred quality; the bond between the two leads to the fulfillment of both. Yet such meanings did not always exist. One seventy-four year old woman remembers a time when children were not associated with intimacy and emotional well-being for parents but rather were understood as an inevitable and difficult responsibility:

> Children were something difficult. Children were something you give up your life to, you devote your life to . . . My parents looked upon us as a responsibility. They didn't look upon it for all the joy and pleasure of children. It was a responsibility, a hard responsibility.
>
> Susan, age 74

This woman's sense of well-being was not constructed as dependent on bearing and rearing children. And she did not see women as necessarily "motherly." When I mentioned today's ideas on women's maternal desires and special mothering abilities, she laughed loudly: "My mother was *not* a nurturing person. You know, it may be true for some mothers. But my mother was just not. My mother had very few mothering qualities. As I say about both my parents, they accepted us as a responsibility." These words are a reminder that not all mothers embody "relational" styles of behavior. Negative economic and social circumstances, changing ideological fashion, and individual personality factors impinge upon and disrupt the idealized version of a nurturant orientation.

Historical fluctuations in birth rates suggest a link between national issues and the perceived desirability of motherhood. During the Great Depression, serious relationships and marriages were postponed and the decision to forgo motherhood seemed appropriate. Under conditions of economic hardship and of formal institutional measures discriminating against married women, avoiding marriage and motherhood was a survival strategy.[25] When I asked Marge, who was seventy-six at the time of our interview, how she accounted for her decision to remain childless (which I assumed to be a highly irregular choice given her age) she answered: "I think of myself as a product of the times." For her, childlessness did not seem at all unusual and was a "very easy choice" to make. Her job was very important to her and all her friends were women in the workforce. Many of them were married and remained childless. For women in her class location, having a child was equivalent to losing a job. Given her experiences as a daughter and as a participant in history, forgoing motherhood was not constructed as a sacrifice. She reports never feeling any internal pressure *to* have a child.

Just as motherhood took on a certain undesirability during the Depression years, employment took on enormous meaning. The four oldest women I interviewed (ranging in age from the late sixties to the late seventies) did marry, but retrospectively they considered their public work, their politics, their creativity and/or their spiritual lives to be at the center of their identities, not their relationships.

The oral histories of women who lived through the Depression highlight the necessity of taking "cohort effects" into account in any discussion of women's psychological development. National issues impinge upon and alter opportunities and transform desires which in turn reshape developmental paths. Women's psychological orientation, far from remaining immutable, appears to be plastic and interactive with the economic and social conditions in which their lives are situated. Whatever the "times" suggest about gender roles, individual women don't simply choose their place. Stereotypes of correctness exclude some women, and thus encourage their sense of difference. I turn to this point next.

Exclusion

Nonconformity was not always exactly chosen: in some instances it was *assigned* because of a woman's characteristics. Deviations from rather rigidly imposed norms of weight, height, beauty, or social grace contributed to early feelings of exclusion and disrupted achievement of a traditional female goal—attracting male attention and approval. One woman, who grew to be 5'10" during her junior high years, told about having to look down at her teachers and the school principal. Another woman, who put on glasses in the seventh grade, spoke of "looking terrible" and always "feeling ugly." Not surprisingly, weight showed up as an issue in several women's stories. One woman described herself as "grossly obese" as a youth. Others described themselves as "overweight" or "chubby." Along with nontraditional desires, for some women not being able to achieve certain norms led to the development of a sense of identity not dependent on being "feminine":

> I was one of those classic unhappy little nerds in the corner, one of those kids who knows she was different . . . Literature was my savior and my release . . . I read books about other women who were different and other women who dared and other women who made up their minds what they wanted and it didn't matter. And those were my role models . . . A lot of the famous Victorian novels are about women who are different from the Victorian norm, and remember the Victorian norm was an incredibly rigid one, what a woman was and what a woman could do and what a woman couldn't do. And they were usually not beautiful, not submissive, rebellious, had their own ideas, wanted an education, and wanted other kinds of things,

wanted to be something more. And the books usually had them winning out in one way or another.

Isabel, age 45

As I started to do this (written exercise) I thought back and I thought about my teenage years . . . It wasn't rebelliousness, but it was always feeling like I didn't quite belong with this group and I didn't quite belong to that group. And when you are a teenager you always try to fit in. And I thought about the turmoil I went through, trying to be A or trying to be B and never quite being either. But sure giving it a try because you want so much as a teenager to be that way. But then as I matured, it wasn't so important for me to be like A or B. I could be C and that was fine too.

Helene, age 48

These recollections can be seen as examples of Clara Mayo's concept of "positive marginality."[26] When faced with not fitting in, women diverged from mainstream views and went on to develop a positive interpretation of the nature and value of their identities. Both strong ambitions to exceed the limits set by gender and being marginalized by narrow definitions of femininity figured—in varying degrees—into individual women's development of nonconformist identities, as "always having been different," as being "off where other people weren't, marching deviant."

Membership in minority communities may also be associated with and provide support for being different. As one woman, a Christian Scientist, said it: "I always made the distinction, there was 'them' and there was 'me.' Being part of a minority religion group, you make that distinction somewhere along the line. I am comfortable being in a minority position. I always was."

Perhaps because many women in the sample were daughters of first and second generation immigrants, their stories stress cultural differences based on ethnic and religious minority status. A more thorough investigation of such difference is not possible here, but it is important to note that ethnic and religious identifications are woven into accounts about difference.

By the time that most women came to consider reproductive options, regardless of the explanations they constructed to account for their noncompliance to the motherhood norm, most reported the experience of remaining childless as just one more example of "being different":

> What you do in life if you are a woman is you get married and have children. But I had already been different about all the other things. When I decided to get a Ph.D. quite early in life my mother and father said, "What do you want to do that for? You know, you can go to be a kindergarten teacher, you could go do that like everybody else." So that was already different . . . So there were already different choices made before against the grain and our marriage was already going to be different and against the grain so not having children was just going to be "strange Isabel" again. I had already mapped out a thing for myself as being not like other women. And it just continued to fall into that pattern.
>
> Isabel, age 45

> I've always felt different about one thing or another . . . I think I was the first one in my family to marry outside of the religion. So not having children only made me feel different for yet another reason.
>
> Helene, age 48

Summary and Conclusion

Childless women's autobiographical musings challenge the notion of a distinctly feminine orientation fixed early in life. Their combined stories provide an alternative view that emphasizes the contradictory nature of women's wants and the role of conflict and resistance in the development of their lives. They demonstrate the non–natural state of current gender norms and highlight the way specific and unrelenting social practices conspire to organize women's interests and activities in particular directions.

The feminist literature on women's development that asserts the centrality of mothering desires and capacities in the constitution of "the feminine" goes a long way in helping us understand and account for women's relational interests and talents. This literature cannot, however, help us understand women's desires for independence and self-expansion or their nonconformist behavior.

The stories that intentional not–mothers tell suggest that early family experience, although certainly central, is not *all–determining*. Their stories lend support to Flax's conclusion that the relationship of individual families to other social institutions needs to be integrated into our understandings of personality development.[27] I argue as well that attention must be paid to the way social practices enforce and reinforce cultural norms. Theories designed to understand women must recognize the ways that women are *pushed* into motherhood, not only pulled psychologically into the role.

A "madness to live" and resistance to constraining forces are not male prerogatives.[28] Recognizing and valuing these dangerous desires and capacities for resistance has implications for women's development and for the feminist movement. Women's psychologies may be understood as sites of differing and often conflicting tendencies rather than as unified entities determining fixed qualities. Relational and autonomous strivings are not moral polarities, one being pro-social and superior, the other being individualistic and inferior. Indeed, connectedness and separateness can be either creative or destructive or both. Social realities lead to conflicts between these tendencies which are found in a complex mix among us all. Women are thus different from and the same as one another; we also change considerably across the life course. In a kaleidoscopic way, desires and behaviors change over time with changing contexts and changing ways of constructing experience. Women cannot escape the power of the ideology of gender, but individuals resist, accommodate, and achieve gender norms in uneven and changing ways, creating multiple identities. And the ideology of gender itself changes. What is socially promoted at one time may be discouraged at another.

The feminist movement competes with dominant patriarchal discourses for the "subjectivities" of women. As feminists we want women to see and resist oppression. Motherhood is *still* a social institution, not a biological or psychological fact. As an institution in a male-dominated society it continues to be oppressive to women regardless of whether we "choose" it or not. Michelle

Stanworth argues that motherhood may be even more oppressive today:

> While women today spend less time in pregnancy and breast-feeding than in the recent past, the care of children has come to be defined in a far more rigorous way; mothering involves responsibility not only for the physical and emotional care of children, but for detailed attention to their psychological, social and intellectual development. Motherhood is seen, more than in the past, as a full-time occupation. Mothers may be expected now to lavish as much "care" on two children as they might previously have provided for six.[29]

Furthermore, we cannot afford, in resisting patriarchal arrangements, to downplay those potentialities in women that threaten patriarchal relations—independent strivings, rebelliousness, non-conformity, assertion, and ambition. The near exclusive emphasis on nurturant and caring potentials will not challenge present social arrangements *unless* combined with these attributes more commonly assigned to men.

In short, the theory and practice of feminism requires resistance to the essentialism through which motherhood dominates cultural conceptions of women. Commonsense values still tie women's moral development and natural fulfillment to motherhood. By inference, childlessness is constructed as ethically suspect and as a loss. But such assumptions involve "attributing particular social meanings and values to the physical capacity to bear children. The 'essential' biological nature of women guarantees the inevitability that we should fulfill particular economic and social functions which may not be in our own interests."[30] The tightly drawn link between women and mothering found in recent scholarly work, without further elaboration, risks obscuring the vast possibilities and actualities that exist within and between women and consigns childless women to the borderland of deviancy. Listening to the stories not–mothering women tell helps make "woman" a more spacious word.

3

"I must admit, I didn't freely admit it"
EXPLAINING THE CHOICE

The distinguishing characteristic of hegemonic ideologies is that they require no proof or argument; their validity is assumed, understood, and ratified by convention, norms, and accepted bounds of respectable discourse. Thus, those who challenge this dominant set of ideas are typically the ones who must bear the burden of proof, a burden that, in this setting, actually defies argumentation and evidence.

—David F. Noble[1]

Sometimes people would say, "Why don't you have children? Why not?" And Frank would say, "My penis got shot off in the Vietnam War." And I thought that was a wonderful way of handling it. I wasn't able to do it that way but we just learned to get less and less defensive and just say, you know, it's a choice we made and we are very happy with it. *You cannot explain that to somebody.*

—Isabel, age 45

CHOICE is a loaded word. The word suggests the opportunity of selecting freely among alternative possibilities. Yet choice depends on what you think or know is possible. There do have to be options indicated.[2] In most research on intentional not–mothers, and indeed in popular discussion, "voluntary childlessness" is a category built on the concept of choice. The assumption is made that women "choose" not to have children; a decision is made, a determination arrived at after deliberation. Among the women I spoke with, the language of choice was problematic. Even when women did experience making a clear decision, the stories they told to account for that decision were complex and inconclusive, open to shifts, reevaluations, and reconstructions. Rather than a choice, or a decision, remaining childless was described as an ongoing practice and/or an outcome determined by a variety of personal and social circumstances:

> With me it was just one actual step leading to another. That's why I don't think it was consciously saying, "We are not going to have children." It was more just a natural part of our way of life and the way things unfolded for us. It was never something we focused on, either in a negative or positive way. We were just doing what seemed right for us and both of us were more professionally-oriented than family-oriented.
>
> Lee Henry, age 66

> I haven't experienced [this choice] as though we're sitting down and making it. It's just been made in terms of how I've lived . . . It's more like I experience it as *not* having made a decision *to* have children rather than having made a clear decision not to have children.
>
> Margaret, age 41

> When Mike and I were married, I was in grad school working on my Ph.D. and I knew damn well, both of us knew, we couldn't afford to have a kid at that point. It was out of the question. And then I had to finish the dissertation . . . And then at the same time we were both breaking into jobs. And so it would have been [pause] Good Lord! And then after that was over with, Mike was diagnosed with insulin dependent diabetes and that was several years where our lives were in absolute turmoil because they couldn't get his sugar level under control. And then, by that time, I was already into hot flashes.
>
> Augusta, age 48

> I was *never* anyone who said, "I don't want to have children." Or wonder if George and I should have children this year or next year. I just always knew it wasn't now. That was fine, and I said, "I don't know, maybe I will." And I think maybe in my 30's it was "maybe I will but I doubt it. Who knows?" And then it just sort of progressed into . . . I will never have children.
>
> Beth, age 44

In these cases, "choice" is a confounding interpretative framework. Childlessness is not understood by these women as a choice but rather as a *consequence* of choosing to live their present lives. Seeing women as "childless by choice" may be accurate at a simple descriptive level. But it misplaces the emphasis and misstates what was chosen. Women are expected to explain a negative occurrence, a negative choice. The absence of motherhood becomes the point of focus rather than the many prior positive choices. What women *do* have is outside the focusing lens. "Childless by choice." The phrase itself signifies lack.

The dominant rhetoric which constructs remaining childless as a choice would construct the above-quoted statements of not–mothers as evidence of "postponement." When women do not make a clear and conscious choice against motherhood, but they remain childless, they become "postponers." Again, the inevitability of motherhood is presumed. It is not surprising that some participants describe themselves with this word. After all, it is the only concept available; there is no alternative construction. Yet one woman did resist this interpretation and in my dialogue with her we can glimpse the possibility of another way of understanding. The exchange starts with Maria stating:

> Narrator: So it was kind of gradual. First, it was temporary decisions not to have children.
>
> Interviewer: So you postponed.
>
> N: Well, we were busy with all these other things. It wasn't like saying, "Oh, we really want to have children, let's postpone." It was more like, "Gee, this is so much fun."
>
> I: Your life was good the way it was.
>
> N: It did not feel like denying ourselves something. It felt like, "Gee, we better use birth control because we can't get ourselves pregnant."
>
> Maria, age 43

This woman takes her present life as her standard. She is not postponing motherhood; she is living her life in a way that gratifies. Another woman rejected the word postponement and asserted she had not put off the decision. Rather, she and her husband had done periodic reassessments about children that always ended in a confirmation of their present practice.

Rhetoric that privileges motherhood is difficult to avoid. Scientific and commonsense discourses describe women as "forgoing" motherhood. The assumption of sacrifice, of giving something up, is embedded in the word and does not capture how a woman feels if her desire for a child is weak or nonexistent. One woman challenged me on my use of the term when I asked her, "How do you understand for yourself your decision to forgo motherhood?"

> Forgo being a mother? There have been so many other things in my life that I don't see it as forgoing because it was a choice that gradually evolved, and it wasn't as if I sat there and said, "I can either be a physician or a mother." I was going to be a physician. Whether I was going to be a mother down the road I wasn't sure.
>
> Ellen, age 43

In some cases, women volunteer to remain childless. Doing so is a second-order choice as, for example, the result of marrying a man who wants no children. In such cases, choice, which implies active decision-making, is not the "felt experience." One woman, married to a man nearly thirty years her senior, states:

> How do you explain the fact that you need glasses? Or that your teeth aren't straight? Or something like that? . . . It's just a fact of my life. I don't even think of it. It wasn't even a decision that I made. There was never a notion of having children.
>
> Cathy, age 45

In two cases, women who defined themselves as intentionally childless had, at an earlier period of their lives, tried to get pregnant. They remained childless by chance, then childless by choice. Claire's story provides an in-depth look at how rigid categories of voluntarily and involuntary childlessness, and chance and choice blur:

> So I got out of high school and went to work a couple of weeks later at a job I liked, doing secretarial work . . . We got married three years later, on my twenty-first birthday as a matter of fact. I do remember

never feeling quite comfortable because I was never quite sure what he was going to do and as it turned out he was an alcoholic and that causes, of course, all kinds of problems . . . We wanted to have kids . . . I mean I wasn't even thinking about it. It was assumed. So we consciously tried to have kids and after a couple of years I had the carbon dioxide in the tubes, I had the dye in the tube, I had a D & C, he was tested, etc. You know, there was nothing wrong that they could figure . . . I remember crying every month, you know, the time you get your period.

After a couple of years, we started to look into adoption . . . Anyway, then the marriage started deteriorating . . . He wasn't coming home at all, he wouldn't go for counseling, and it just wasn't working anymore. So I went to a lawyer and got him served with papers, served him myself as a matter of fact . . . I just couldn't take it anymore.

I went back on birth control pills because I figured I better not get pregnant . . . So that's probably the first conscious decision not to get pregnant. Except, of course, before I was married. So that marriage ended and I decided to start college. I remember one of my first courses was a course in women's studies and they made me tell them a little bit about myself, and I said, "Well, I'm at the end of my twenties, the end of my marriage, the end of my rope!" The feminist movement was coming into its own, the 70s . . . So it was a very supportive time to go out on your own because there was so much going on and I felt having been married and having been divorced no longer had a stigma.

(Then I met my second husband when I was thirty-one.) We got married the end of '76 so I was thirty-four. There was a pretty strong bond right from the beginning . . . I was crazy about him. But I wasn't going to get sucked into anything that was going to make me miserable. I was very cautious, but very open, unafraid of saying, "I don't like this," or "I need this," or "tell me what you're talking about, don't shout, talk to me." Things that I wouldn't have thought doing the first time, making demands.

At the time of the interview, Claire had been married eleven years. I asked if she had considered having children in this second marriage. I asked, "Did you try?"

Kind of. No. Okay. There's a lot of things to consider. First of all, we were not in a financial position we felt. Nobody can ever afford kids.

Right? But we were doing conscious thinking and our conscious thinking said, "we're not in the position to have kids." But before we got married we had 98% decided that we weren't going to have kids, we talked about it. I remember saying a couple of times, "If you think there is the remotest possibility that you want a family, I'm telling you that the possibility of me changing my mind is so remote." And he thought about it and said, "Well, if you do change your mind and we decide to, okay, but if not, that's okay too."

I asked if she was contracepting:

Yes, absolutely. I mean I was as sure as I could be in my mind that I wasn't going to have kids. But who knows? Did I make that decision because I figured I wouldn't meet anybody to have kids with? Did I make that decision because I figured when I met Carl I thought, "I don't think we're going to be stable soon enough?"

I responded: "One thing I wonder about. In your first marriage you describe an intense desire to have children. In your second marriage, you are rather determined not to have children. What changed your intense desire?"

What the hell changed it? My circumstances changed it. Absolutely. I still like kids, I would still like to work with kids. I think it was sheer circumstances and I don't think it was anything else . . . The circumstances being a lousy first marriage, uncertainty at the beginning of the second. And by the time the uncertainty went away, the ability was still there, but I think we decided we were having too damn much fun. If I had got pregnant, would I have had an abortion? I think I probably would have. Again, we talked about this . . . and I'm pretty sure that by that point it was "I'm too old." You kidding me? A baby? Relying on one income? We bought a house. No. All the things that you have to change to accommodate a child. The tradeoffs are too great now and the desire for a child, it's a total turnaround . . . After we were married for four years, and we weren't going to have kids, and I had to get the hell off the pill, I had my tubes tied. I don't remember any anguish over it. It was like the decision had been made years earlier.

Claire, age 45

Another woman's report points to the problematic nature of categorical thinking that separates "voluntary" and "involuntary" childlessness. Edith and her husband were patients of Masters and Johnson and tried for years to conceive a child. At the same time, she thinks of herself as intentionally childless, as someone who didn't really want children. "I think I did it just to sort of, I mean, I'm not going to make huge waves, I'm not that kind of person." She sees her behavior as appeasing everybody in the family and she relates her inability to get pregnant to her psychological resistance. Is Edith "childless by choice"? No—and yes. Yes—and no.

The discourse constructing voluntary childlessness and involuntary childlessness is reductionist. The words choice, postpone, and forgo are simply too limiting to contain the historical processes that many women describe. The rhetoric is maternalist as well: it presumes women ought to be mothers. The language used to describe this group of women whose childlessness is multi-determined not only misinterprets women's experiences, such language disguises the political issues surrounding childlessness. It is within this rhetorical context that women who define themselves as childless by design are called upon to explain themselves.

Explanatory Work

For some women, the attempt to construct and articulate the origin and development of their childless status proved difficult, if not impossible. Although their life stories suggested many factors, when confronted with the point blank question, "How do you understand your decision to remain childless?" they were unable to provide an answer.

Helene is a woman who never desired to have children. "It was nothing like entering marriage with the thought that we would have children, and then some point along the line decided not to. We entered marriage knowing we would not have children. And I can't tell when or how that came about. We did not drift into it after we were married." I asked her how she understood this early stance:

I don't know. Because in my career I've always had something to do with children. I was at one time a teacher and I've always been in some form of work where I have had to deal with children. I don't know why, back those many years ago, I said I don't want any for me. We are not the kind of couple that does a lot of partying or a lot of social life where I might have said I don't want anything to interfere with this. Because we have never been that way as a couple. So I really can't tell you why I would have made the decision.

Helene, age 48

Marge described herself as "never the domestic-type person. Never occupied myself with thoughts of a home which seems to be built into a good many women." She tried to explain but had difficulty doing so:

I expect I just don't understand myself. I seem not to have had a natural urge to have children. I like children and I have nothing unhappy in my own life to make a decision not to have children, but it just didn't seem to be in my make-up to want to build a nest and lay eggs I guess. And I'm more interested in what's going on. I'm interested in government and what makes the world tick.

Marge, age 76

In these cases, women's attempts to explain themselves involve a process of rejecting the stigmatizing explanations which are part of the cultural landscape but which do not correspond with their experiences. The popular understandings of why women remain childless are revealed with great clarity in their statements: First, such women do not like children; second, they are self-centered; and third, they had unhappy childhoods or unhappy life events of some kind that led to their nonreproduction. Such negative and universalizing generalizations are common and reveal the persistence of the assumption that normal women or good women want to be mothers, that desiring motherhood is "natural." Only women who are morally suspect or flawed by events beyond their control would reject motherhood.

The above accounts reveal more, however, than the fact that not–mothers are maligned. When dominant ways of constructing their experience are rejected, some women are literally at a loss to explain. Yet women are forced to speak, as relatives, friends, and acquaintances (and of course researchers) ask for explanations. Without a discourse in circulation that equally privileges not–mothers and mothers alike, childless women often maintain their integrity through various verbal negotiations. In some instances their words may be no more than a vocalized silence:

> At a very early age I knew what I wanted and I did it. But I didn't, I must admit, I didn't freely admit it. I mean I didn't advertise it. And a lot of people simply don't ask. The years roll on, oh, people did ask. "Well, you've been married two years." That was the standard. That was it. "You're not pregnant?" And then I would say, "Well, you know, it didn't happen yet" . . . I wasn't totally honest . . . If I had announced it or declared it or made a thing of it, it probably would have offended people.
>
> Carole, age 55

Carole is now a stockbroker who "formed the idea" that she did not want children at the age of seventeen. "I was just horrified by the lifestyle. It was just total slavery as far as I'm concerned." She was determined to remain without children and negotiated this as a condition before agreeing to marriage. During our conversation, Carole spoke of her hunger for adventure and the freedom to pursue a wide variety of experiences. Yet this information about her was hidden from others as she did her best to survive in the hostile climate of the 1950s. Lee Bishop, ten years younger than Carole, also remained silent about her intentional childlessness when she was young. "I kept quiet about it in those days. We told people we were saving to build a house." One wonders how many married women throughout the centuries were pitied as sterile when, in fact, they intended a life without children.

Another way several women protected themselves when faced with a curious and potentially unfriendly audience was to use humor. "We treat the questions kiddingly." Women avoided serious answers (if indeed they had constructed them for themselves). Humor is a way of remaining silent and is useful in situations where inquiries are experienced as "people getting on your case." One woman shared her standard line: "Oh yes, we had kids but we sold them so we could travel." She added: "If somebody just asks out of curiosity and it's a non-offensive person, well, then that's okay . . . Now if the attitude is you should have had kids, then you get no information from me, my back goes up."

Another woman I interviewed typically used a one-line response to the "how come?" question. "This is just how it worked out for us." "Because this is what we chose." Lee Henry's responses shut down rather than open up the subject. She uses these statements when she perceives danger in speaking publicly about her lack of interest in mothering.

Remaining quiet is understandable. Not so long ago, in 1972, Shulamith Firestone asserted that it was physically dangerous for a woman to come out openly against motherhood on principle. "She can get away with it only if she adds that she is neurotic, abnormal, child-hating, and therefore 'unfit'."[3] Silences are reinforced by routine etiquette. For example, in a 1988 issue of *McCall's*, Charlotte Ford advises a woman who is asked why she and her husband don't have any children yet to answer, "'Oh, that's a very personal matter,' and move on to another topic of conversation . . . such sensitive issues really aren't suitable subjects for small talk."[4] Unfortunately, as Catharine MacKinnon says, "One genius of the system we live under is that the strategies it requires to survive it day to day are exactly the opposite of what is required to change it."[5] The reality that not all women want to be mothers remains hidden, reinforcing the "natural" connection of women with mothering.

Not all women used strategic silence to deal with predictable queries. Some did just the opposite. They went into great detail to justify their behavior and to win the acceptance of others. One woman used the language of war and spoke of the necessity of defense and her ability to "disarm" the questioners.

> I do find that one of the greatest defenses when you get into these situations that, you know, always happen from time to time, is that people will say, "oh, you don't have children?" and they have those little downcast looks like, "oh, you poor thing." And I'll say, "Well, I

really like children, I work with them all day frequently," and I go on and on, I mean, I know so much more about children than most of the people that have them and they are like "wow" and I talk about the relationships we have with all these various nieces and nephews and so on so they are just like so surprised at all this that you've really kind of disarmed them so that they can't really come at you with any kind of routine.

Louise, age 45

This woman works hard to illustrate her liking for children and her involvement with them in order to disarm the assumptions of those who question her. A political reading of her statement might see her in a struggle for power in reaction to the lack of power she experiences vis-à-vis mothers. This is the same woman who speaks of feminist ideology as providing "cannon fodder" in her attempts to validate her status. Again, the language of war is used as this woman prepares to "defend" herself when she hears the question, "do you have children?" and, as she ages, "how many children do you have?"

Another participant spoke of having gone for years through "a long song and dance" trying to justify her behavior and become acceptable in the eyes of others. Such strategies to gain power are at best partial because they depend on the concession of power by the questioner. As this woman gradually became secure in her non-conformist position, she found that by reversing the assumptions of the dominant discourses that marginalized not–mothers, she took power rather than waiting for it to be conferred.

One way women can affirm their childless status in language is by reversing the prevalent meanings of "mother" and "not–mother." This reversal of discourse is often labeled as defensive or as overcompensation, discounting the attempt to present a different reality. Chris Weedon reminds us, "Resistance to the dominant at the individual level is the first stage in the production of alternative forms of knowledge."[6]

Not–mothers' reversals offer a self-respecting identity from which they can speak. By reversing meanings they participate in the redefinition and reevaluation of what is considered natural for women. And they produce explanations which are both personally affirming and politically challenging to the dominant interpretations of childlessness as loss, as absence, as the vacant opposite of motherhood:

> I don't need children to fulfill my life. I guess if you needed a reason, that would be my reason. I don't need a child or children to feel complete.
>
> Ann, age 59

> We were both very busy with our professional lives . . . There was no time or void that we felt that needed to be filled . . .
>
> Lee Henry, age 66

> I want it all and I got it all and I'm saying that consciously. And I'm saying it again, I've got it all. No, I don't have kids but I've got it all. It's different, but that's all it is, I'm not missing nothing. You're always missing something. I've never had a Cadillac. I've never had six cats. I've had two husbands, that's enough!
>
> Claire, age 45

Prevailing ideology validates particular types of individual satisfactions, pleasures, and self-fulfillment for women—primarily those connected to children and men. Other sources of gratification for women are denied, especially if they are pursued in lieu of children (or men). These women reverse any assumption of deficiency. They present themselves as complete, fulfilled, as missing nothing. It is this challenging speech of not–mothers that contests the received interpretations of what childlessness means for women.

The fact that women are called upon to explain themselves and must develop strategies to cope with the "eternal questioning," as one woman put it, documents the existence of power inequities and conflict between mothers and not–mothers, parents and not–parents.

> It is the people who *have* children who say, "Oh, don't you feel a great loss?" It's not the people who don't have them. When I wasn't married, it was always the *married* people who were trying to marry me off. I was obviously suffering some terrible deprivation. (Laughing.) I don't know, misery loves company, I guess . . .
>
> Ann, age 59

Strategic silence, disarming the questioners, and reversing the discourse are verbal responses used when women are called upon publicly and must involuntarily account for their nonconformist behavior. But the burden of explanation is felt not only vis-à-vis others. For some women, a considerable amount of energy is expended trying to explain to *themselves* why they remained childless. One woman spoke of her twenty-year struggle to construct an accurate understanding of her clear and strong rejection of motherhood before marriage. In her statement she acknowledges the fact that more energy may be spent in the future on this task:

> When we were engaged we were talking as you so often do about children's names and we started saying, "Well, here are some great names." And at one point we looked at each other and said, "Wait a minute. Why should we necessarily have children? Do you really want to have children?" And we both decided at that point that we didn't. And we've never veered away from that again. Now, there are some particular *reasons* for this that took us a very long time to figure out . . . I think only in the past few years do we really have a full sense of the many different factors that influenced us, and there may still be others that we are still not aware of.
>
> Isabel, age 45

Four years after my original interviews, I contacted participants, sent each a nine page research summary report, and invited their responses. One woman wrote: "I continue to reflect on factors that account for my being a 'non–mother.' Here are some of the 'new' insights I have had." A full page of hand-written notes listing three insights followed. Her insights involved conversations she had had with her husband—one nine years ago, another twelve years ago. And the third insight involved her husband's conversation with an adoptive mother. For the purpose of my discussion here, the content of her perceptions is less important than the *process* she reports engaging in, the emotional/intellectual work of trying to figure out how, in fact, she has ended up without children.

In summary, women are called upon to explain their nonreproductive stance to others; they may also wrestle internally with understanding their not–mothering preference. They do so in a generally unsupportive social milieu. The anecdotes in circulation about intentionally childless women are not ones that emphasize the courage and strength of nonconformists. Rather they are stories of pathology, loss, regret.

Given an unsympathetic or insensitive context, women developed ways of protecting themselves when called upon to explain. Yet they had to do so in a language that legitimates motherhood even as it automatically constructs their own lives in terms of deficiency. The words commonly used to describe their reproductive status and process take the desirability of motherhood for granted and take motherhood as norm.

"Childless by choice" is a liberal concept that reinforces mothering. The word choice fabricates the individual subject as an autonomous entity with rights to privacy and personal happiness. Such a notion emphasizes personal decisions and distracts attention away from the social relations of power. The insistent focus is the internal as opposed to the institutional and sociopolitical.[7]

Alternatively, when one conceptualizes childlessness as an ongoing social practice, its study leads to an inquiry into the circumstances under which women remain childless. Looking further into the substance of women's accounts sheds light on such circumstances.[8]

A Working of Injustice

"You must choose between your art and fulfillment as a woman," the analyst told her, "between music and family life." "Why?" she asked, "Why must I choose? No one said to Toscanini or to Bach or my father, that they must choose between their art and fulfillment as a man, family life . . . Injustice everywhere." Not where it is free choice. But where it is forced because of the circumstances for the sex into which one is born—a choice men do not have to make in order to do their work—that is not choice, that is a working of injustice.

Tillie Olsen[9]

Rather than having a clear and easy answer as to how or why they were childless, many women I interviewed identified multiple and various factors throughout the course of the interview. Women's routes to childlessness as they described them were complex and varied, encompassing psychological and social explanations. And although a great many factors influenced their nonreproductive stance, experiences with and beliefs about patriarchal motherhood played an especially important role. Critical interpretations of the conditions under which most women must mother were nearly universally expressed. Motherhood conflicted with desires for economic and emotional autonomy and self-expansive activities.[10]

For many, the assertion that women cannot mother without costs to themselves—costs this group was not willing to pay—was grounded in their own experiences of nuclear family life and in their perceptions of the experiences of others. The older the woman, the starker the forced nature of her choice, as historical circumstances pushed married mothers out of public life and into a dependent reliance on a man:[11]

> My sister was married at 18. My father pushed it, my father arranged it. And I didn't like this. By the time I was into my teens, I was already a rabid feminist. I was already fighting this. No man was going to do that to me kind of thing. I liked men, I dated, I could picture myself getting married. But I was going to be an independent person and children, you see, didn't fit into that pattern because having a child would mean I would have to be dependent on somebody else . . . Being a mother would throw me into a situation I didn't want to be in. Of being dependent on a man and having to be subservient and giving up my life . . .
>
> And before we married, I made sure. I talked about this. I felt he had to know how I felt about children and home because if he didn't agree with me it would be a disaster. I was not going to marry a man who wanted the kind of wife who would be a homemaker and mother. And to marry a man under those circumstances and have him discover it afterwards would be just disastrous. It just would not be right. It would be terrible for both of us.
>
> Susan, age 74

Susan, retired and living with her husband at the time of the interview, worked most of her adult life as a chemistry professor. She sought the jobs she wanted and when the occasion called for it, she established her own residence apart from her husband.

For some of the women in my sample who were in their mid fifties and beyond, the idea of having important work of their own and also being a mother was not perceived as an option. The do–both ideology so promoted today was not in the air.[12] There were no public discussions of parental leave, child care needs, or expectations of co-parenting. These women equated having children with leaving paid employment and staying at home, a sexual division of labor, economic dependence, and the erosion of their power within marriage.

For younger women, those now in their forties, there was not the same assumption that motherhood precluded self-defining and paid work in the public world. Yet this fact created a new set of dilemmas that was equally troubling. Participants could not imagine assuming responsibility for a child or children and being the *kind* of student or scholar or artist or architect that they wanted to be, nor the *kind* of mother they felt children needed. One woman, a Ph.D. who was the first in her family to complete high school, put it this way: "I cannot do justice to a baby and to a doctorate." Woman after woman described her deep commitment to whatever responsibilities she accepted. Nearly all participants in the study had very high standards, not only for paid or creative work but for mothering as well. In short, most of these middle-aged women were cynics about "having it all" on their own terms. Isabel, who is an independent filmmaker, put it this way:

> I'm one of those people who doesn't believe that you can do all those things (motherhood and career) equally well and everybody turns out all right. I think that's a fantasy, I think it's a delusion, the superwoman thing. I think somebody loses. And who loses may well be the child, maybe the husband or the kind of relationship you can have as well as you with your sense of guilt and trying to give everybody an equal share. And I never wanted to do that. I always wanted to have a career that meant a lot to me and Frank and I always had this relationship that

meant a lot to us. And we figured that would be 100% right here. And it is without a child, who should be the first priority.

Isabel, age 45

I guess the pendulum swings. Of course in my generation, those few women who were geared towards a career felt that they had to make a choice. It didn't seem possible for a woman to make the choice of having a career and having a family. Whereas somehow young women within the last few decades have been led to believe that they can have everything, the superwoman kind of thing . . . We had to make hard choices. And our choices at the time were either career or children. Maybe marriage, maybe even not marriage. And as I have told you I would have seriously considered no marriage then. And that meant living a pretty celibate life because you didn't have relationships very easily at such a time.

Susan, age 74

One woman, when I asked if she could imagine both having her career in the social services and a child, responded:

No, because as it is I try to be superwoman in that I try to do the best I can in all areas whether it's doing something at home or doing something at work and when I was going to school that was another component. And I know that if I had children I would try to be supermom and I can't be all things to all people.

Helene, age 48

Women who remain childless thus challenge the seductive "do–both" ideology that emerged in the late 1970s. This ideology, which does not demand that men "do both," serves the interests of a capitalist economy as it promotes the notion that women *can* take on the unpaid work of caring for children and home and still flourish in their careers or creative work. Many women in my sample had a clear sense of "motherhood as institution" and what the institution means for women. Rather than fulfillment, doing both motherhood and self-defined work was viewed as an impossibility, a "set up" leading to frustration and failure and loss. These women were clear about the lack of supports available to them. Co-parenting was not perceived as a viable option by most women given their husbands' lack of enthusiasm and/or demanding employment. Even in those cases where co-parenting was believed possible, women remained skeptical that such a private arrangement would provide enough support:

> We have neither what we could get in Sweden nor what we could get in a traditional situation. And that's it. It's you and your husband, totally . . . And then there is the ethic of buying out. And you get some undocumented Salvadoran to come in, she leaves her babies on the other side of town. And many people we know are getting into these relationships, and I understand that's what people have to do. But I think it's a bad way for people to move. I think day care is a terrific idea, but it's the minority people coming into your home that makes my skin crawl. On the other hand, I can understand . . .
>
> I think our family structure is too small to support us. And that we need to reorganize it. And if we did, then people wouldn't have to make such stark choices. They wouldn't be put up against the wall and have to buy out in certain ways that are probably very difficult for them.
>
> Margaret, age 41

> If I had a large number of supportive family members, I might be able to pull it off. But, you know, not by myself. Not with just Mike and me. That was something that was real clear to me.
>
> Augusta, age 48

Scholars in various disciplines argue that conditions for mothers have gotten worse, not better. Following changes in work and family structures, the onus on women in terms of child care and good mothering has increased.[13] The care of children is defined in a much more rigorous way than in the past. North American mothering now involves not only tending activities but detailed responsibility for the child's intellectual, psychological, social, and physical growth.

Emotional time and real time become major factors. For example, Donna talked about spreading herself too thin. "I mean, even with all the supports you still have to supervise them. You know, if the child is sick you still have to be torn between being in two places. I don't know. (Pause.) The other thing that pops to mind too is that a marriage is a real commitment. I mean what's the sense of being married if I'm going to have a job and a bunch of kids and not have time for my husband, or he for me?"

The problem is not one of work versus family life alone. The problem extends to having time to do other things as well. Women wanted personal time and time to devote to friendships, political and volunteer work, avocations, athletics, whatever. At the present historical moment when women are encouraged to take on "ever greater amounts of work and manage ever more contradictory demands on their time,"[14] and accept ever greater stress in their day-to-day lives, one woman spoke for many when she said, "no way, I can't do it all." With few exceptions, the workings of injustice, either implicitly or explicitly, escorted women's desires to remain childless.

No Call to Motherhood

Of course, even in the perfect post-patriarchal world, where women are not penalized for becoming mothers, women who are not interested in bearing and raising children would exist. Participants' choice accounts challenge more than structural arrangements. Some accounts contradict the maternalist ideology upon which such arrangements depend. "My experience was that even if I examined the best circumstances with a mother and a child living in the best possible world, it still wasn't that appealing to me. I just wasn't moved towards it." Following are additional testimonies that call into question the "naturalness" of women's desire to mother:

> I never had the desire to have children. Never. I don't have any maternal instinct whatsoever and it makes me wonder if I am abnormal in this total absence of desire . . . I've never felt that motherly urge, or whatever it is. I have no idea what people are talking about when they say that. In fact, my co-worker just became a grandfather and was showing me pictures of his new granddaughter today and I had to really force myself to say, "oh, isn't that cute" or pick out

something nice because I really am not child oriented. I did babysitting for a little while, but I didn't particularly like handling kids, especially little kids. In fact, I have three nieces, and I enjoyed them more when they became old enough to be able to respond vocally and to talk and interact with me. So, I don't know, whatever that motherly instinct is, I've never really felt it, or never really felt strongly about it.

Sally, age 45

It was a decision I made at age sixteen. It just never came up again. I only discussed it when we were getting married to make sure, you know, I'm marrying somebody who goes along with this because I know I don't want children. Clearly there's this absence of instinct totally. I just don't have an iota of it. I'd be curious to know if that's the case with most of the women you interview or not . . . Maybe you can tell me that from the people you've interviewed, is that typical?

Carole, age 55

There was never one particular point when I said, "Oh, I'm going to be childless." . . . Many people have asked me this, oh, you know, you are so good with kids, ta ta ta, you should have children. So one is always forced to confront this question I think in this society. I don't think I *ever*, even as an eleven, twelve, thirteen year old, I *never* had that "I've got to get married and have a family." I don't ever really remember a point in my life where I felt like I had to have a family. And when I think about the conversations I've had with many friends, how high that figured into their hierarchy of needs, it just wasn't an issue for me . . . I had an abortion when I was about 35 or something. It was the only time that I had ever become pregnant and it just wasn't the right time and also I didn't want to have a kid. And so, you know, that was a real conscious choice. It was interesting because I was real clear about it.

Louise, age 45

When it really came down to saying "are we going to do this or not?" I really didn't *feel* like doing it. I never reached the point where I felt that this was something that I wanted to do. I assumed for many years that it would be something that I would want to do—later. That I would see that moment and at that moment it would be clear to me and then we would do it.

Jo, age 43

Karen Lindsey, called upon to write an article for *Sojourner,* a feminist periodical, echoes the words spoken above in her article, "Middle-Aged, Childless, and No Regrets":

> The problem for me in writing an article about why I don't want children is the same problem I faced fifteen years ago. I don't have any great complicated, philosophical excuse for not wanting kids—I just don't want them, in the same way I don't want to live communally or move to Florida or listen to punk rock or become a surgeon . . . I can't argue that I'm torn between kids and a career—at the time I decided to get sterilized I didn't *have* a career.[15]

The above women are European–American. But not having a call to motherhood has been reported in other studies done about childless women. An African–American woman speaks in the pages of Susan Lang's book, *Women Without Children.* Candice tells us that "I have never, not even for a second, ever wanted to have a child."[16]

Such unexpected statements, if not psychologized away, offer a political challenge to the idea that the desire to mother is inevitable for women. Not all women experience conflict about remaining childless; it simply is never a felt need. For some, the social organization of mothering influences desire. For others, disinterest in child tending and caretaking activities figure prominently. Some women don't see themselves as doing interpersonal relationships well. In still other instances, women feel they have already been mothers to younger siblings and lack the desire to mother again. In these cases, women's talents and inclinations simply take them into unassigned territories.

Whatever the reasons, taken as a group, the women I interviewed constructed having children as a loss of present gratifications and future possibilities. Thus they reversed the taken-for-granted *meanings* of motherhood and childlessness. Motherhood is perceived as the negative condition, characterized by loss. Remaining without children is the affirmative practice.

Summary and Conclusion

According to the prevailing cultural assumption, it is natural for married women to become (and want to become) mothers. It is within the context of this ideology that women who are childless by design are called upon to account for themselves. Women who are mothers are not under the same pressure to explain their reproductive behavior because its "validity is assumed, understood, and ratified by convention, norms, and accepted bounds of respectable discourse."[17]

Such explaining proved difficult for the majority of women I interviewed. Commonly constructed as a choice or a decision, few women actually experienced childlessness as such. Rather, the majority of not–mothers described a long, complex historical process that culminated in living permanently without children. There were many explanations, many variables, related to changing circumstances. Even though their behavior remained consistent, i.e. no children, some women reported ongoing reconstructions of why this was so. For some, it was difficult to understand oneself, much less to try to explain oneself to others.

Taking into account cohort effects, the older women interviewed were subject to greater social coercion and therefore their "choices" were more constrained. The choice to mother meant the choice to leave their careers. For younger women there existed a social expectation that self-defining work and motherhood could coexist with little loss to either role. This expectation followed structural changes in the society. However, "doing both" was not perceived as an option by these women; without adequate supports, they could not imagine taking on both tasks responsibly.

Remaining childless does not occur simply in a private realm. As Cynthia Fuchs Epstein summarizes it:

Although there is a widespread belief that the desire for children is either an inborn or an early acquired trait, the community and the state rarely leave to individuals the right to decide whether to procreate or not—in the same way that the society does not leave gender distinctions or the division of labor to chance . . . Thus, the so-called natural and private consideration of people to become parents, or more particularly, of women to become mothers, has always been intruded upon by persons outside the immediate family.[18]

Although women's reproductive choices are usually considered to be primarily emotional, Susan L. Williams reminds us that such choices involve not only unconscious conflicts and family history, but also the "social, political, and economic history of patriarchy and oppression."[19]

Again, Berenice Fisher reminds us that personal history and the history of patriarchy intermingle.[20] Reproductive choices are highly conditioned by a multitude of factors, including family history and cultural heritage, material conditions, the political and legal conditions of the historical moment, and a woman's own physical and mental health and the health of those close to her.

As circumstances change, choices may also change. For all women, reproductive technologies, economic downturns, a movement for gay and lesbian parenting, an unintentional pregnancy, "a change in the legal status of abortion, success in finding a long-sought-for partner, the death of a sibling with children, growing involvement with work, a mid-life crisis—any of these things might affect a woman's choice to have or not have children."[21] Further, for some women, desire for children coexists with resistance, given their circumstances. Desire and disinterest are both present as the practice of childlessness continues. Unapologetic childless women, consciously or not, defy a culture, an ideology, a language which structures female life around the male and around childbearing and childrearing. The next two chapters consider the symbolic implications of such defiance for women's daily lives.

4

"She thought I was some kind of ogre that eats children for lunch"
SYMBOLIC POLITICS I

The personal and subjective struggle of all oppressed people is one against being defined as inferior, marginal and deviant, in the language, discourse, myths and fantasies of the dominant culture.

—Lynn Segal[1]

You know, I still am Barb. I still can be a whole person without having to mother, having to carry an infant around full-term, you know. I *can* be somebody. And, in fact, I am.

—Barb, age 43

I N popular consciousness, childlessness is regarded as an affliction.[2] In a world where womanhood is synonymous with motherhood, and motherhood is seen as both moral obligation and ticket to fulfillment, this comes as no surprise. Historically, childless women (along with a variety of others who deviated from prescribed gender roles) have been subject to a "rhetoric of rejection,"[3] the use of stigmatizing labels that exclude them from the category of good woman. Since a good woman experiences fulfillment through nurturant activities, and the intentionally childless woman is presumed not to be nurturant, the labels are unpalatable: "selfish," "unfulfilled," "regretful."

Clinical psychologist Jane M. Ussher suggests a general method of disempowering such contemptuous stereotypes: first, carefully examine the discourses framing women's experiences; and second, offer alternative explanations that break the frame.[4] The project of the next two chapters is to apply Ussher's model to disagreeable images of nonreproductive women, to examine the discourses that frame them as deficient women, and to hear childless women's responses in order to provide conceptual alternatives to the customary rhetoric of rejection.

To begin, I return to the European–American history of symbolic distinctions drawn between mothers and childless women.[5] Second, I identify and discuss three specific rhetorics or discourses constructing childless women that, taken together, maintain the symbolic boundary between mothers and childless women: discourses of derogation, compensation, and regret. I weave into the discussion not–mothers' responses to these stubborn thought patterns and I rename their experiences in order to break the standard frame. As the reader will see, some women worked hard to resist being passive receivers of popular clichés, others did not. But they all found ways to intercept and reconstruct the received meanings of the symbolic order which claimed to describe their lives.

Historical Context

As discussed in the introductory chapter, the symbolic distinction between mothers and childless women we experience today is deeply tied to the extraction of women's unpaid household labor. Scientific support for the collapse of woman–into–mother was produced in the nineteenth century in Britain and the United States by primarily white, upper-class professional men who argued against the growth of women's higher education and participation in public life on the grounds that their reproductive powers would be diminished and their offspring damaged. As summarized by Jane M. Ussher, "the brain and the uterus were conceptualized as being in competition for vital resources and energy, so that to concentrate one's resources in one was to deprive the other."[6] The natural "uterine" woman could be assured of a happy destiny while the "mental" woman, who developed her mind and shunned bearing children, could "only hope to be a freak, morally and medically."[7]

Such theories, Ruth Hubbard reminds us, were used to disqualify women of the doctors' own class and race from professional competition while securing their attentive services as mothers, wives, and sisters. Significantly, these new doctors of obstetrics and gynecology, biology, and psychology "did not invoke women's weakness to mitigate the exploitation of poor women working long hours in homes and factories that belonged to members of the upper classes, nor against the ways African–American slave women were forced to work for no wages in the plantations and homes of their white masters and mistresses."[8]

Toward the end of the nineteenth century, middle-class and wealthy women began openly challenging maternalist ideology, creating a crisis within Victorian society: "not only was the future of the species in question should women reject their natural destiny, but individual women were likely to suffer from madness, insanity and destruction."[9] Women who questioned their role as childbearers and wished to assume the rights of men were labeled as "hysterics," as "petty tyrants," as "malingerers," who were attempting to avoid their womanly responsibilities.[10] This group of women was, for the most part, non-procreative and sought independence and a career of some kind. Neurologist Horatio Donkin, one of the most progressive doctors of the time, ultimately concluded that hysteria was the result of frustrated sexual and maternal drives rather than the result of societal influences.[11]

Thus the subversive desires of women of a certain class—their ambitions that had nothing to do with motherhood and caretaking activities—were defined as evidence of illness. And women who indulged these improper desires were threatened with images of being or becoming mentally, morally, or physically sick. Indeed, given these societal pressures and constraints, for some women these warnings became self-fulfilling prophesies.

The social control of women's reproductive lives continues into the twentieth century. Ussher contends that real world opportunities for women have expanded since the 1960s, "but the internalization of the idea that fulfillment for women is through childrearing and consumer spending" remains as powerful a force restricting women as were the nineteenth century treatises by male psychiatrists.[12]

Today, when many women "do both" childtending and participate in the paid labor force, women are still socialized into looking toward motherhood for identity and fulfillment. It is acceptable for a woman to "do both," but women who "do only" a vocation or an avocation that excludes motherhood are continually chastised and warned about distressing real or potential consequences of going against the grain. The updated version of the good woman/bad woman split defines the good woman as mother, whether or not she has a career.[13] The bad woman, who deviates from the reproductive norm, becomes the unmotherly "career woman," who is portrayed as dangerous, unhappy, perhaps even deranged.

Much contemporary feminist thought either intentionally or inadvertently participates in this symbolic splitting. As detailed in the introductory chapter, influential feminist writings from the late 1970s into the 1990s have emphasized the particularly female qualities of caring and relatedness. In much of this recent work, women's independent longings and activities are critiqued as individualistic and male-biased while the nurturant qualities of women are celebrated.[14] Of course, not all feminist-identified theorists support "modern maternal mythology."[15] At the extremes, the feminist scholarly debate is between maximalists, those who magnify the attributes traditionally associated with women, who see women as having a "distinctive orientation," and minimalists, those who minimize gender differences and thus point to qualities and interests assigned to men that are found among women. Maximalists comprise a strand of feminist thinking sometimes referred to as "difference feminism."[16] As the reader may have surmised, I stand closer to the minimalist tradition.

Two examples serve to illustrate that maternalist thinking can be found embedded in feminist thought on either side of the minimalist/maximalist divide. In the June 1987 issue of *The Women's*

Review of Books, Anita D. McClellan favorably reviews cultural anthropologist Patricia A. McBroom's book, *The Third Sex: The New Professional Woman.* McClellan summarizes how McBroom, in studying female managers in the corporate world, defines successful women as working mothers, and failed women as childless:

> In the population McBroom studied, some of the women with unresolved issues of power occasionally avoided marriage and always rejected motherhood outright. Others pursued unproductive relationships and inadvertently postponed childbearing until it was too late. She terms both groups culturally maladaptive because of their childlessness: sacrifice of childbearing by more than half of all professional women in America—intentional or not and dictated by the nature of the work world *as much as by women's own weak gender pride*—is symptomatic, says McBroom, of a *severely traumatized population.*[17] (Emphasis added.)

What McBroom labels "the third sex" is the relatively small, "culturally adaptive group" of women who have combined motherhood and career successfully. "For the Third Sex, 'femininity—the sense of comfort and satisfaction with feminine roles—was not at war with professionalism.' All the careerists wanted to be mothers as surely as they wanted to excel professionally."[18] McBroom correctly criticizes an inhumane and patriarchal corporate world, yet by labeling childless women as culturally maladaptive, she makes motherhood mandatory. McBroom also assumes women should adapt to patriarchal arrangements.

In a collection of essays that appeared in 1990, idealizing norms of motherhood are exposed and explored. The editors of *Ties That Bind* address the oppressive complexity of the mothering role and critique maternalist thinking. This collection acknowledges the contributions to child nurturing by women other than biological mothers and has much to recommend it. This is *not* a work that reifies motherhood.

Yet the first few sentences of the introduction to the volume disturb my comfort as a childless woman. "Motherhood is arguably the most profound life transit a woman undertakes, the deepest knowledge she can experience."[19] This may be arguably true for some mothers. But is having a child the central transformative experience for all women who are mothers? In part, because of this ideology, mothers who find their centers elsewhere do not freely and easily advertise their reality. If motherhood is, indeed, the deepest knowledge a woman can experience, childless women are forever excluded from women's ways of knowing. How can we be real women? If I were asked what my most profound life transit was and the deepest knowledge I have experienced, of course motherhood would not be my answer. But I would have an answer; it would just be a different response. Yet if motherhood remains the *deepest* knowledge, whatever I construct will be shallow in comparison.

How can interested feminists undermine the symbolic distinctions that frame mothers as somehow superior and childless women as inherently flawed? The point is not to attack mothers. But such symbolism is worth dismantling as it oppresses both mothers and not–mothers alike. One way to begin is to critically evaluate the symbolic boundary separating mothers and not–mothers by identifying specific discourses that construct the boundary and by listening to childless women who do not fabricate deficient identities nor experience childlessness as a cross to bear. Their voices, while neither idealizing nor denigrating a life without children of their own, can widen the parameters of "possible selves"[20] that women may morally claim.

As I talked with the women in my sample (and later read and reread their words) I listened for their stories of childlessness. Together we discussed the ways in which childlessness is constructed in the dominant society and narrators provided alternative constructions. The "big picture" posits mothering as the primary and best role for women and childlessness as its vacant yet negative opposite. Three dubious discourses about childless women help paint this portrait. They are the discourses of *derogation* (these women are morally flawed); *compensation* (not–mothers' activities and attachments are simply efforts to make up for the absence of children); and *regret* (the only future for the childless). Derogation and childless women's responses to it are the subject of this chapter; compensation and regret are discussed in the chapter that follows.

Derogation

CATHY © 1987 Cathy Guisewite. Reprinted with permission of UNIVERSAL PRESS SYNDICATE. All rights reserved.

Maternalist thinking links motherhood with female moral virtue. Mother love is an extraordinarily powerful symbol for the most selfless kind of human practice. Indeed, motherhood, nurturance, and self-sacrifice are made synonymous through language; when women act in caring ways towards people other than their own children, they are often described—and describe themselves—as acting maternally.

But this connection between mothering and concern for others has unfortunate consequences for women who intentionally remain childless, as the above cartoon demonstrates: If women don't care for children, they care only for themselves.

In common discourse it is the act of having children which defines the family. While "single-parent family" is a common term, we hear little of "no child family." And if having children is pro-family, then not having them becomes anti-family. In this era of "family values," few charges are more to be feared.

In political and moral debates, family values are socially responsible and selfless. The rejection of family values is identified with the selfish materialism of the marketplace. One way the moral meanings of motherhood are created and sustained is through stereotypical representations of intentionally childless women and couples as self-indulgent consumers.

The media promote a picture of the carefree, well-off and heavily consuming childless couple. "What Do DINKS Do?" asks the

Niagara Gazette. "They don't have kids but they love their lifestyles."[21] Highlighted are two "double-income, no-kids" couples, one photographed with their pets, the other drinking wine in their luxurious home. Consumption is the theme: "They *admitted* their lifestyle includes a lot of material things like boats (one for pleasure, one for water skiing), cars (a sporty convertible and a GEO Tracker), cruises and vacations in Mexico."[22] (Emphasis added.) Upper and middle income couples without children may indeed enjoy the things their money can buy. But, of course, not all childless couples have comfortable incomes or consumer orientations. And although most wealthy adults are also parents, media articles that interview them about parenthood don't focus on their materialism.

A moral boundary has been constructed between parents and not–parents. It is fictitious. It is constructed by what is emphasized about not–parents (selfishness) and what is not emphasized about parents (selfishness). The border distorts reality and it ignores class and societal issues. Yet it remains a cultural force to be reckoned with.

The association of childlessness with selfishness was well understood by the women I interviewed. All were familiar with the common stereotype of the married woman who acts against motherhood as a self-centered, ungiving person.[23] One narrator explained that when others ask if she has children and she replies "no," she "wonders if they are thinking sterile or selfish? How are they working it?" This is the social construction of childlessness in a nutshell.

Not surprisingly, few participants saw themselves in this light. Most often, the link between childlessness and inappropriate self-centeredness provoked strong reactions. As one woman said, "there are ways to give other than motherhood." Dominant meanings were countered as women engaged in reversing maternalist thinking, giving moral testimony on behalf of themselves *and* other not–mothering women. Some women felt that because of their childlessness they were able to reach out to others in ways that mothers might find difficult given their family responsibilities. In the examples below, women reclaim their right to be seen as

ethically-sound people and describe the nonfamilial forms their giving assumes:

> I think one of the interesting ironies is that sometimes people will say,
> "these must be selfish people because they don't have kids." And yet,
> when I look at the way we live, in many ways, we are not at all into
> what people would expect us to be like—heavy consumers, privatiza-
> tion, the couple together, being selfish whatever they are doing. But
> we have quite the opposite, I think, reaching out all the time which is
> identified with families but it's often not the way most families func-
> tion right now where you have this turning inward.
>
> Louise, age 45

> I'll tell you, I think you are more thoughtful of your friends and are
> more concerned with other people and their problems because you
> don't have children. I think you are a more concerned person because
> somebody that has children has got their hands full right there taking
> care of problems.
>
> Marge, age 76

> I don't think we deserve the label "selfish." We are very giving when
> it comes to our time and efforts and support for our students and our
> universities. I think our universities are so lucky to have us because
> they can count on us to do things way above and beyond what most
> faculty members are willing to do because we don't have children.
>
> Maria, age 43

> The only thing I care about is that I lead my life in a way that doesn't
> harm future generations. I am as worried about the planet as if I had
> children. I think for a lot of people, and you hear this in the rhetoric
> all the time, that people do things on behalf of their own children,
> that people's social conscience is derived from simply guilt from
> doing wrong to their children. My feelings are not oriented toward
> any specific child or person. It's more that all people should be able to
> enjoy life.
>
> Jo, age 43

Certainly most narrators resented their exclusion from the high
moral ground reserved for mothering women. One woman's comment summarizes for others the central reaction: "My capacity to
love, I don't think, would be increased if I had kids."

Defenders of patriarchal attitudes disagree that no moral difference exists between women who do and women who don't
become mothers. And so does an important strand of feminist
thinking. Since difference feminism has gained in influence over
the past two decades, some feminist writers have assumed the position of border guards keeping female virtue safe for mothers.
Not–mothers disappear from the moral center. Feminists contributing to the new mothering literature may see the association
between moral behavior and motherhood as socially constructed
rather than natural. However, the link itself is reasserted.
Motherhood, rather than an *expression* of women's pre-existing
nature, becomes the *origin* of maternal behavior.

Sara Ruddick is perhaps the most visible scholar writing about
the connection between motherhood and ethical behavior. In her
book, *Maternal Thinking: Toward a Politics of Peace,* Ruddick elab-
orates her thesis that mothers develop special qualities such as
concern for others, a healing orientation, and cooperativeness. It is
the social practices of mothering which lead to special values and
behaviors that may provide the basis for a nonviolent world.
Women can and do develop their capacities for caring when they
become mothers, and Ruddick appropriately attends to valuable
personal and social outcomes of the mothering role. But her tight
connection of pro-social behavior to motherhood raises as well as
answers questions. Are women who do not tend children less
responsible to or concerned about human well-being? Are there
sources of healing orientation other than childrearing? Are all or
most mothers so peace-loving? Does the universal experience of
mothering render economic and cultural contexts inconsequential?

As a social worker I have worked with poor mothers so overwhelmed by the demands of socially unsupported parenting they
were unable to practice compassion towards their children. I have
also met middle-class women who violated their children's bodily
and emotional integrity in their efforts to guide and protect them.
Katha Pollitt, writing in *The Nation,* suggests that Ruddick might
have studied health professionals, whose work involves saving lives,
for a loving, nonviolent constituency. "Or I don't know, gardeners,

blamelessly tending their innocent flowers? You can read almost any kind of work as affirming life and conferring wisdom."[24] Further, Pollitt questions Ruddick's move from a mother's care for her child's well-being to an assumption that this care extends to all children:

> But mothers feature prominently in local struggles against busing, mergers of rich and poor schools, and the placement of group homes for foster kids, boarder babies and the retarded in their neighborhoods. Why? The true reason may be property values and racism, but what these mothers often say is that they are simply protecting their kids. Ruddick seems to think Maternal Thinking leads naturally to Sweden; in the United States it is equally likely to lead to Fortress Suburbia.[25]

The risk in Ruddick's analysis is reinforcement of traditional antinomies: female work is healing, male work is harm-doing. Men who assume female work as childcarers are able to get to the high moral ground, but women who don't won't. The symbolic boundary separating mothers and not–mothers is reinforced and given feminist and scientific legitimacy.

In my sample I found women who were socially active and women who weren't; some who viewed themselves as selfish, some who didn't; some identified as pacifists, some not. Some women described material pleasures and others had little interest in them. None, of course, are mothers. "I'm probably a little selfish but I think most of us are. But, I mean, are most people willing to admit it?" Rhonda related her reluctance to take on motherhood to her inability to maintain "a certain amount of unselfishness" that she believes is required:

> When I was in college I remember girls talking about having children and whatever. The whole idea of it just never, I could never get excited about it. Never, never said a thing to anyone, but I couldn't understand. There was a part of me that could not understand why all that responsibility would be so attractive to anyone. Because I think I look at it in terms of a monumental responsibility . . . I see it as a certain period of years until the child's at least eighteen, you have to

be . . . it's not just "me." It's essentially me and the child or hus-
band/wife and the child. So there is a certain amount of unselfishness
that's necessary.

Rhonda, age 48

Here selflessness *is* connected to mothering. Yet in my sample it
is clear that not–mothers engage in unselfish work and develop
their life-affirming skills in social practices other than parenting.
Indeed, peace-oriented social activists I spoke with saw the absence
of children as a direct contributor to their ability to act on their
social commitments:

> Since I haven't had children and I haven't really had to put personal
> activities on hold because I was taking care of them and keeping
> things together for us as a little social unit, I've been able to develop
> myself as an individual and as a political person . . . I have hopes that
> my political work could be something that is life-affirming in another
> sense than having children . . . I think that if I'm very successful, I'll
> be able to do something for kids . . . and to make it into a more
> human world.

Margaret, age 41

I would not argue that childless women are essentially socially oriented because they are childless. But the social practices of
childlessness may reinforce caring behavior which simply takes a different shape from that practiced by mothers. Not–mothering
women's caring may take a less privatized form, necessarily less intertwined with biological ties. This is illustrated by my participants'
plans for their estates. The importance of social class will be obvious.

Parents leave their property to their children, almost universally
and automatically. Childless women disrupt this reproduction of
class patterns associated with inheritance. But the women are not
busily and selfishly spending everything now, or writing wills leaving everything to their cats. Rather, without excluding relatives and
friends, their plans emphasize cross-class giving primarily through
commitments to public need.[26]

Among the women I interviewed, the beneficiaries most often
mentioned were charitable organizations or institutions of impor-

tance, such as churches and colleges. A number of women spoke of setting up special funds or scholarships to help others who had financial needs:

> I've written a will . . . Well, I have a scholarship fund for women. I mean, I think not being able to go to medical school myself . . . I have some young women who I've known, they've gone to college and so forth and they are just trying to start careers and I'm leaving some to them. And then to some causes like Amnesty and things like that.
>
> Elizabeth, age 48

> Oh yes, I have a trust. The beneficiaries? Charities. Animal welfare. The university. And the hospital. And Planned Parenthood. I left my jewelry to a friend who I had met in the Army . . . And I left my car to a cousin. They will probably predecease me so I think as an alternative plan I would give household goods and anything like that to the battered wives shelter.
>
> Ann, age 59

> We have charities that we feel very strongly about, and our estate is set up with the charities and groups that we particularly like. For example, I read a great deal. So, we designated money to our library association. My husband's active in the Animal Rescue League. He's been their treasurer and vice-president for years. So that's another charity . . . We're very comfortable with the choices, the disbursal of the estate. And that gives its own pleasure. Like, "oh good, this will be good for them and that will be good for them." Items that are precious to us are designated in the will to friends.
>
> Lee Bishop, age 45

Human beings are capable of selfish and selfless acts. The moral high ground and low ground (however defined) are not limited to one group or another. All humans engage in both self-centered and other-centered practices. Certainly socialization and social circumstances are associated with variations in behavior, but labeling women's positive impulses as maternal and connecting them (and them alone) to mothering simply reinforces negative stereotypes of women who don't mother. Mothers and not–mothers both lose, one trying to live up to an impossible model, the other trying to live an undesirable one down.

An important question remains to be asked: Just what constitutes selfishness? What the terms selfish and unselfish mean socially is impossible to know with any precision, which allows users to attach their own meanings. Anthony Cohen reminds us that often the contents of categories are so unclear that they exist almost exclusively as symbolic boundaries. Thus, the issue here isn't really the issue of morality. This may really be a matter of reproductive control. Cynthia Fuchs Epstein says it well:

> Control . . . may be exercised at the micro level, at not always perceptible levels, although it is true that people may often be clearly aware that words, like symbolic behaviors of other kinds such as rituals and ceremonies, are instruments, tools, and weapons to erect walls or bring them down. At base, language itself creates boundaries by providing the terms by which real or assumed behaviors and things are grouped.[27]

In the case of this symbolic distinction between mothers and childless women, the behaviors are *assumed* and the substance of the moral difference is of little importance. Even so, some women I interviewed had to struggle with internalized versions of their moral inferiority in order to gain comfort with their childlessness.

Coming to Terms: Negotiating Derogatory Discourses

> I feel like I nurture a lot of things. It's like I didn't give up that part of me. Mothering is just a very small part of the whole picture. I think when I got that clear for myself, that it was okay, I wasn't going to hell for it [remaining childless] and I wasn't going to be a shriveled up old lady for it or anything else, it was like, if it's good enough for me, that's good enough.
>
> Barb, age 43

No participant entirely escaped the impact of prevalent negative representations of childless women. Some women negotiated these beliefs and images easily and without struggle. As one woman put it, "I knew it was out there (the idea of not–mothers as selfish) but I said, you know, this doesn't apply to me at all." For other women it wasn't quite so effortless. Negotiating popular ideas required a series of adjustments over time, through which women consciously replaced disapproving views of childlessness with affirmative visions of themselves as nurturant and ethical women.

As is evident from the previous chapter's discussion of explanatory work, not–mothers engaged in "reverse discourse" in their social lives. Women employed this same reversal process to deal with their interior lives. Most women, sooner or later, easily or with great effort, had to "come to terms" with subjective fears about the meanings assigned to them by the culture. One woman related her "coming to terms" episode, which involved seeing her whole life in a different light:

> I can't remember exactly when this happened. But I remember standing in the kitchen thinking about it. I remember thinking, "Oh shit. I am such a neat person and there are so many things that I know and all this is going to die with me. And I have missed the chance to create a little person who thinks like me and looks like me and acts like me and can keep doing the same stuff I'm doing. So all this experience that I've got and these hip understandings that I have stop here."
>
> Then I began to think a little more rationally and I began to think, now wait. If the only reason that you would want to have a child is to create somebody who looks like you, thinks like you, and is going to be brainwashed into your image, then it's a doggone good thing you didn't have a kid!
>
> And I realized, shoot, as a teacher I'm passing on great stuff all the time in the classroom . . . And then, my sister has a daughter who is eleven and I am absolutely the most perfect eccentric aunt. And I love that role . . . For several days after that, I would be recognizing things that I would be doing as, "Yes, this is the way I'm passing on my ideas and yes, this is the way I'm sharing my expertise, and yes, this is one of the proofs of this understanding I have come to." This stuff that I was normally doing I was seeing in a different light. *I'm seeing it as an act of nurturance* and perpetuating my ideas and things like that. (Emphasis added)
>
> Augusta, age 48

In this episode, Augusta confronts the deeply ingrained cultural assumption that women best nurture and give permanently to the world by becoming mothers—and the implicit assumption that not–mothers are deficient givers. She comes to terms with her childless status by claiming an image of herself as a loving person whose own life will be perpetuated in the lives of nonbiologically related others. Such a claim is antagonistic to maternalist thinking.

Women reversed the received knowledge about childless women as selfish or uncaring. What was trickier and did not lend itself to a simple reversal was the religious charge of immorality. Close to one-third of the sample of women I interviewed were raised in the Roman Catholic Church. Two women joined religious orders for a period of time before they married. According to the church, sex is permissible for the purpose of procreation. Women who marry and intentionally remain childless while intentionally being sexual defy the fundamental moral order. It is not always easy to go against God, but women found their ways.

One of the clever ways that women negotiated deficiency discourses was through expropriating traditional religious symbols or beliefs in support of their disobedience to religious rules. One woman used God Himself (sic) in order to override her Catholic guilt. Her story necessitates a brief contextual statement. Barb, the woman quoted at the beginning of this section, spent two years in a religious order before marrying. Her husband, a man with a physical disability, made it clear before marriage that he would not risk biological parenthood and passing along a genetic disease to a child. This was not initially a problem for Barb. After a couple of years she grew increasingly uncomfortable about being married without motherhood. She and her husband considered various reproductive options and finally decided on artificial insemination. On the weekend before her scheduled appointment to be inseminated, Barb and her husband imagined a situation she describes as "the turning point" in accepting herself as an intentionally childless married woman:

> And we were going back and forth. Is this the right decision? Is this the wrong decision? Should I or shouldn't I? And so we talked about it and we batted it back and forth. And I remember pacing and saying, "I just wish God would come down and enlighten me. I just

want a bolt of lightning." And Joe started chuckling. He said, "Let's pretend. If Jesus or God was in this room, He'd probably have a beer in hand and He'd be pacing with us" . . . So I visualized God just pacing with a beer and turning around and saying, "Barb, you know, it really doesn't matter. Do what you need to do, you know. I don't think any more or any less of you." And once I visualized this Greater Being say, "I don't have anything invested in this. If you do it, do it because you want to do it—for yourself." And it was then that I thought, "If it really *is* my decision to make, well then, no" . . . And I think for me that was the turning point . . . I don't need to procreate to be okay.

Barb, age 43

Barb creates a loving and permission-giving God to replace an authoritarian and judgmental one who would punish her for her moral transgression. She draws on selective religious imagery to undermine constructions of a punitive "Greater Being."

Another woman playfully resisted the morally inferior identity assigned to her by the Catholic Church and her Latina culture by applying a key religious and cultural belief to exonerate herself of reproductive wrongdoing:

Narrator: As we say in Spanish, "Lo que Dios me provea." "Whatever God provides for me . . ." There was a feeling that if you're suppose to have a baby, then you'll have a baby regardless of how well you take care of yourself . . . or how many birth control pills (you take). I mean, if you forget one, if it's there for you, you're going to have it. If it's going to be, it's going to be . . . That's very cultural.

Interviewer: You did contracept though?

N: Yes, because I wasn't quite ready for God to provide (laughing). I kind of set the conditions for God providing. I never forgot to take my little pill.

Gloria, age 43

Later on in the interview, Gloria, laughing, said:

If God wanted me to have kids, I would have them. And obviously God did not want me to have them. So here I am. Justifies a lot of things in your life, you know it. External controls are wonderful in certain instances. You don't have to deal with any guilt. It's not my fault.

Gloria and others refuse to be disciplined by powerful religious ideology. Women turn the tables on oppressive religious discourses by using those same discourses to protect themselves from its censure.

The image of the deficient childless woman might be a myth, but myth itself is a powerful reality.[28] The coming to terms stories of married not–mothers demonstrate the resourcefulness women show in negotiating those forces which act to maintain the present moral order.

The intentionally childless women I talked with knew others might think of them as selfish because of their not–mothering status. They also were aware that others often thought of their activities and interests as compensations for missing children. An additional attitude was especially threatening: you will regret your decision. The next chapter investigates compensatory discourses and this life sentence of regret.

5

"The thought, 'will I regret it when I'm old?' is impossible to avoid . . . because it's just out there"
SYMBOLIC POLITICS II

Somebody just recently asked about my grandchildren and I said it was not possible because I didn't have any children. And they said, "Oh, I'm so sorry." I wondered about what.

—Lee Henry, age 66

Compensation

COMPENSATORY discourses make motherhood the natural condition for women by describing the activities and attachments of not–mothers as compensations for the original deficiency, *no child*. Every aspect of a childless woman's life may be interpreted through the lens of this deficiency. These discourses make central what one does not possess, what one has not done. *Whatever* a childless woman *does have* or *does* may be viewed as merely compensation for the missing real experience of motherhood. Motivations to achieve, active public commitments, avocations, relationships with pets, are commonly interpreted as evidence of the inevitable void left by a failure to mother. Of course, comparable activities and attachments among mothers are not viewed in this fashion.

One narrator alerted me to the fact that "the notion of compensatory means that there is a standard that you're not meeting." She spoke of the oppressive nature of such an assumption:

People talk about us as whatever we're doing is compensatory. The reason I'm working so hard is that I'm compensating for not having children—that's the oppression and being ostracized. And I do get a lot of that. "She works all the time, no wonder she publishes all that. I wouldn't like to be like that. I wouldn't want to be so single-minded because that's not a balanced personality."

Elaine, age 48

Many women I interviewed found that others saw their lives as simply making up for the lack of children. The following words of one of the participants points to this experience:

Most people are overwhelmed with the number of things I do. Now, of course, I guess you could say that, "Oh my God, of course she does all this as a way of compensating." Well, I mean, after a point, if the person wants to believe that that's the case, what can you do? But I don't think of it as compensatory. I like to do these things. I'm a real active person. I have certain values and I want to make those active in the community, so I get out of my doorstep. But it's not like a compensation for me. Maybe the cat is the compensation, I don't know, maybe the cat . . . (laughing)

Louise, age 45

Indeed. What about the cat? Women's relationships with animals provide a forceful example of how compensatory ideology works. A prevalent cultural view is that among the childless, attachments to animals signify a substitution for the missing child. One woman told about the "cute and sweet" way her husband's father inquired about their parenting plans: "Is this the best you can do, kitty cats? Roger's answer was 'yes' and that was that." The media, a powerful agent of socialization, is fond of promoting this thought pattern. The language and images of child-substitution abound. For example, in 1991, a picture of the Duke and Duchess of Windsor appeared in *The Buffalo News* with the caption: "The Childless Duke and Duchess of Windsor with their Child-substitute."[1] (Why not "The Duke and Duchess of Windsor with their Canine Companion?") A 1988 "Francie" cartoon pictures a childless heterosexual couple sitting on a park bench talking to a mother with two children. The childless woman is holding a dog on a leash; the dog is dressed in frilly baby clothes. The man is saying to the mother, "How did you know we didn't have any children?"

Given the common nature of the symbolism, it isn't surprising that some narrators who had deep bonds with four-legged creatures often defined their interspecies love as maternal. Even so, women were always clear that they enjoyed the unique relationship that develops with animals for its own sake. It had intrinsic merit. Pets were pets, not replacements. But narrators were conscious of compensatory thinking and did contrast pets with children. They spoke in good-natured, humorous ways, sometimes even announcing a preference for animal companions over child companions. One narrator's letter with photo that I received a week after our phone interview demonstrates the centrality that pets can assume on their own terms:

> The only other thing I would like to add to our conversation of last Saturday is about my dog, Sally. She is so black that you can only see her brown eyes and her Christmas ribbon in the photo of the three of us. Sally is a very important part of my life, and Ed jokes that in the event of a fire I will save Sal before I will think of him. She is ten years old and very loving, playful, a big tease and she is obedient. If there is any shred of maternal needs within me, I lavish them all on Sally. Having a dog is so much better than having children—we don't have to hire a babysitter if we go to the movies, she doesn't play loud rock music, she doesn't bring her sloppy teenage friends over to mess up the house, and she is always in a good mood.
>
> Kay, age 46

Another woman I interviewed is nicknamed "The Mother Theresa of the Animals" in her rural community where she engages in animal rescue work. When I asked Ruth if she could identify any ongoing theme in her life, she reflected briefly, then spoke: "Probably the love of animals. I just really love animals and I always have." She talked about the advantages living with animals has, given her strong commitment to her architectural business:

While the commitment [to animals] is very strong, it's a commitment that you can leave for the day and still come back and they love you just as much and you haven't lost anything by not being with them. They haven't lost anything. But I think a child needs to—especially when they are young—they need continuous attention and they need continuous development to be the people they need to be.

Ruth, age 43

Women I interviewed were familiar with the ideology that turned pets into replacements for missing progeny, and, for the most part, rejected it. Lee Bishop loves her cats, "they're fun to watch, they're fun creatures," and she often jokes about them being her children. But she doesn't think of them as substitutions for children. "They don't require as much care. I often laugh about the fact that my children can stay in the garage." Below is a dialogue I had with Helene who lives on a farm with many animals. Our conversation addresses the issue of substitution theory and it provides the reader with an inside look at the common identification and comradely relationship between researcher and narrator in this study:

Interviewer: Do you ever think of any of your pets as child substitutes?

Narrator: (Pause.) I've been accused of it because they all have people names. But I don't treat them as children. They don't wear little clothes and they don't sit on little chairs. And I don't think I spoil them any more than other people who have children spoil their pets. I don't talk to them. And I don't refer to myself as "Mommy" and I don't refer to my husband as "Daddy."

I: (Pause.) So it may be something that is in other people's heads, not yours?

N: Yes I think so. Yes.

I: Larry and I used to kid about people's children being plant substitutes because people would notice how we cared for and appreciated our plants, nurtured them if you will, and people would make fun of us and our plants. So when friends would say, "well, maybe your plants are children substitutes," we would say, "well, maybe your children are plant substitutes."

N: (Laughing loudly.) I like that! I like that!

When I asked one narrator, who was cat–identified, if she viewed her cat as somewhat of a child substitute, she directly challenged the assumptions underlying such a view:

> That's based on a premise that you need a compensation. You know, that something is missing so you are trying to fill it in and for many of us that isn't true so it's maddening to see it that way. I don't feel that there is any compensation needed. But I like to have some other living thing in my life. And the plants do that as well. And I certainly don't see them as child substitutes. I like to see life and growth all around me. And I like the interaction with an animal. But that's a different kind of interaction than you have with a kid that you take full responsibility for twenty-four hours a day . . . I like to watch a cat's grace and everything. As buddies, as fun, as a companion when Frank's not there . . . And that's a whole different aspect from the mother-child relationship.
>
> Isabel, age 45

For those women who did have animal companions, the bond was generally quite important—it enhanced their happiness. Women wanted the special enjoyment that human–animal relationships can bring. Cara has always nurtured animals. Before I had the opportunity to ask about pets as child substitutes, she revealed the commonness of this belief:

> And it's not really a substitute, but we've always had some kind of a pet around. And right now I have a cat that adopted us, and we took in a couple of dogs that people didn't want and lavished affection on them too because they need a home, like this cat. She really adopted us. And I had her spayed and she's a real pet. So you have something to lavish your love on.
>
> Cara, age 78

Plainly said, many women who did not want a child did want a relationship with an animal. "On those days when you've had an absolutely miserable horrendous day or the whole world is going wrong, having someone who loves you is just great . . . I can get that from my dog. Pets are not judgmental, they're always there for you."

During the course of my research, a veterinarian, who had read an essay on childlessness I had written, contacted me for more information about my work. She is a woman who has never been interested in motherhood. I sent a draft of this chapter and invited her response. Below she offers her view:

> The idea of a need for surrogate children is preposterous. I am a veterinarian. I have animals at home. So do many families with children. Interspecies relationship is part of an enriching, holistic approach to life. It places human beings and their significance on earth into a relative perspective instead of according dominion to one single species over all others. It teaches respect of others and of earth's life cycle. Without this respect our own species will become extinct.

The idea that childless women form attachments to pets because children are absent legitimates children as the proper target of women's caring and reinforces the belief that women need to be mothers. Women's real and direct interspecies bonds are not taken on their own terms but become symbols of deprivation and the unfulfilled need to mother. Such symbolism is rarely if ever applied to the many adults with both children and pets.

Of course, not all people without children are interested in animals or have pets. Diana Burgwyn, author of *Marriage Without Children,*[2] found no substantiation of the view that childless people are attached to their pets as child surrogates. I think it is doubtful that married couples without children have pets in any greater proportion than married couples with children. Indeed, within my sample, women were as likely to eschew pets, given their desire to minimize domestic responsibilities and maximize flexibility, as they were to enjoy pets.[3] "We had a pet once upon a time and the reason we didn't get another pet is because we don't have time for the pet. It's selfish to put a little pet in that condition. I mean, to get a little dog or a little cat or whatever and leave him by himself in the house, that's cruel . . . I don't have time to stay home with him and bond (laughing)."

One effect of compensatory discourses is that childless women begin to feel that they *do* need to compensate for the fact that they

are not mothers. In my sample, several women spoke of the need
to achieve something special because, if all else fails, they could not
fall back on motherhood to provide status and a sense of accom-
plishment. Some narrators felt that others are more understanding
if you are doing (or have done) something outstanding with your
life. This created internal pressures. One woman expressed it this
way: "If you don't have kids, then hell, you'd *better* have achievements that compensate." Deena, a physician, facetiously said, "Oh
I think they just think I made the decision (to be childless) because
I'm a *doc*-tor. Being a *doc*-tor overrides all that. You have a *ca*-reer,
doc-tor. That's obviously almost as good." Almost, but not quite.
And Elaine said:

> Partly what's happened is I've been able to carve out a life that's val-
> ued, so that I'm a Ph.D. All the other criteria that others evaluate you
> on I've done alright on. So I have something to say to them about
> who I am.
>
> Elaine, age 48

In summary, the evaluation of childless women's activities and
relationships as surrogates for motherhood enforces one life path
for all women—a path where a child of one's own is the natural
object of love and where the care of one's own children is the central activity. Women who do not meet this expectation are
compared to those who do—and evaluated on those terms. Even
to make the care of nonbiologically related others central, through
various public activities that do not include childrearing, is seen as
second-rate. The privatized nuclear family is the privileged site for
women's time and attention; a committed public life is an inferior
substitute.

Perhaps if motherhood were not so massively privileged as *the*
central source of gratification for women, a wide range of satisfactions equal to motherhood would be legitimated, making the
option to forgo reproduction more thinkable. But not without further change. Compensatory thinking is a minor irritant compared
to rhetoric that sentences childless women to a lifetime of regret.

Regret Sentences

Certainly the thought of "will I regret it when I'm old?" is impossible to avoid, that sentence even, because it's just out there. So I think I've said, "Gee I wonder if I'll be sorry when I'm older." But it doesn't have any power for me right now.

Beth, age 44

We were married in 1969, and we made the decision right before we were married . . . And in the first few years we were married we had strangers and friends actually stopping us and asking us, "When are you going to have children?" And when we said, "Never," they'd say, "What do you mean? You are going to regret it."

Isabel, age 45

I've always got a lot of satisfaction in my life from my friends and from all my activities and the teaching that I do, so all those kind of generative activities that I would suspect that most people get from raising their children, I get from other things. I don't know, I mean, people say, "Oh, you will wake up at seventy or something and you will regret this." Maybe this is the case, I don't know. But I certainly know women in their 60's, 70's, and 80's who didn't have children and have pretty happy lives.

Louise, age 45

Emotion vocabularies serve social functions.[4] Emotions "are constituted and prescribed in such a way as to sustain and endorse cultural systems of belief and value."[5] For the purposes of my analysis here, I follow the lead of Rom Harré, social scientist and philosopher, who suggests that a useful question for me to ask is: "How is the word 'regret' actually used in this culture?"[6] My specific concern is how and why the word is used in the reproductive arena.

The statements of not–mothers that appear above clearly demonstrate the fact that regret is an emotion assigned to the childless—an assignment impossible to escape. Motherhood, by contrast, is rarely associated with regret, a cruel word implying pain rooted in fruitless longing. Women considering motherhood do not have to reckon with discourses that threaten them with future regret if they become mothers. The notion that childless women, as they age, will look back and lament their decision, acts as a powerful reproducer of the ideology and practice of motherhood. Indeed, threat of regret is one way that pronatalism is promoted. As one contemporary novelist suggests in her book, *Baby-Dreams,* women today continue to be moved in the direction of childbearing, in part, to avoid the panic and fright they feel at the prospect of remaining childless.[7] In short, the message that continues to predominate in the culture about not–mothers is that we *must suffer* for our decisions, for stepping out of line.

The texts of intentionally childless women provide little evidence that women suffer from ongoing or serious feelings of regret. Most women who were adamant about remaining not–mothers described whatever regrets they did have as they aged as tied to their work lives. Women spoke regretfully about various facts, such as missing the opportunity to go to college right out of high school, of having to postpone graduate work or of giving up the dream of medical school due to lack of money, or of leaving academia for the corporate world. Most didn't regret not having children; many never desired to have children in any strong way. Rather, what many women did describe was ongoing comfort and reinforcement of their childlessness over time, along with occasional "rumblings"—times when childlessness erupted into consciousness for reconsideration or review. And a few women shared stories of emotional upheaval with the transition of childlessness from a temporary to a permanent status.

"Dead Forever"

At twenty-three and thirty and thirty-two (pause) I know there were points where I checked in on the decision. And at thirty-two it was dead forever. Even as a discussion in my own head.

Sara, age 46

For those women who had an aversion to or no interest in motherhood, their childless status remained comfortable. Carole, age 55, said, "I never had a coming-to-terms experience, I just knew I didn't want them." Lee Henry, age 66, stated, "I never really felt that I had made any kind of mistake." Helene, age 48, thought it is important for those going through reproductive deci-sions to know that they won't regret it later. "If it *feels* right, chances are you won't regret it." After years of being on birth con-trol pills, Sally, now 45, felt no regrets when her husband decided to have a vasectomy years ago. "I didn't have any regrets about it and I still don't. Maybe I'm strange."

Women talked about childlessness becoming more and more settled with passing time. External pressures to reproduce ceased as women aged. And their partnerships, creative work, careers, and activist commitments became strong centers in their lives. As one woman put it, "it has been a matter of constant reinforcement in a sense." Numerous women used the word "reinforcement" to describe their experience of childlessness over time. "It just gets more and more comfortable, like sinking into an old shoe."

I really don't share the experiences that women have who reconsider their decision at certain ages in their lives. It's like once I made it, it was forever made. And it never came back to haunt me in any way . . . The struggle that goes on for so many years for some women, it baf-fles me sometimes because I am not a part of that and I haven't been a part of it.

Susan, age 74

You know, I have such a hard time identifying with people who have decided to have kids but I also have a hard time identifying with peo-ple who have had to struggle in deciding not to. I'm not saying for me it was an easy choice. But it was a clear one by the time it got made. And it's one that seems to have validated itself as the years have gone along.

Jo, age 43

I could never have done this really bold and crazy thing that I did in 1979 and said I'm getting out of academia and I'm getting out of Cleveland. We are going to Seattle and start brand new lives no mat-ter what. If we had had children they would have been hostages to fortune and we would have had to stay and we would have said, "Well, we have the security. How can we give it up?" You can't take risks in the same way. So, it has never been a matter of more or less comfortable, it has been a matter of constant reinforcement.

Isabel, age 45

I think women worry about making the decision . . . By the time it's irrevocable you are so comfortable with it, because if you weren't comfortable with it you would have had a kid somehow.

Claire, age 45

Claire explained her contentment with her not–mothering status as being a function of her personality. "I'm perfectly content with how things turned out. Would I be content if things turned out differently? Probably, because I usually am. So I think it's one's personality, however a personality gets set—environment, genes, who the hell knows."

For Margaret, social context was the key to her comfort with being childless. Her statement lends support to Sharon Houseknecht's notion that reference group support is often more important than the culture's pronatalist proddings.[8] The following is an excerpt from a letter Margaret wrote to me after our interview. The emphasis is her own:

On reflection, I think the most important reason that childlessness is not a source of unhappiness for me is that, as a woman who is a left activist intellectual, I get a lot of approval as I am from the groups that I seek recognition from. Instead of having the question as to why I'm not raising children coming up constantly in my interactions with others, I hear enthusiasm that I am able to participate in political and intellectual activities . . . Essentially, what I am arguing is that all the personal proclivities, experiences, and just plain chance occurrences which led up to me becoming 40+ without having had a child *and not feeling any particular unhappiness over the fact* should be understood, I believe, in the context of my social environment, which is fairly indifferent to whether or not I bear and raise children, and at the same time actively values a level of participation which would be impossible to maintain with a young family.

Margaret, age 41

One of the oldest women in the sample stated that her decision to remain childless was "one of the few things in my life where I absolutely have no regrets." And another woman in her seventies spoke of her reproductive choice as "the best choice I've ever made," since many of the things she valued about her life she saw as directly related to that decision.

Writing in *Off Our Backs,* Carole Anne Douglas repeats the non-regretful stance of narrators when she says:

> So how does it feel to be 45 and not be a mother? It feels much the same as not being a China scholar, another career option that I seriously considered. In other words, I feel that bearing and raising a child was one of the interesting possibilities that I decided against because I chose another focus . . . I thought it might be interesting to women who are making the decision to hear from someone who does not regret her choice.[9]

In short, regret is not an accurate descriptor. All but one narrator rejected the label "regretful." The designation seemed too pervasive, deep, and enduring to describe their experiences. Instead, women tended to relate specific occasions when they experienced "wistful" feelings, or unsettling "rumblings," or "twinges" of doubt, or "passing thoughts" about the road not taken.

Rumblings

Death or illness of a family member could be one such occasion for second thoughts. One woman's experience is illustrative. Her certainty about her decision was shaken with the premature death of her husband:

> If there was one time when I really had remorseful feelings it was after my husband died. And you see he was only 56 and I was 51. And honestly, we were so used to each other, gosh, when you think of it, from the time I was 16 and all, we were each other's world . . .
>
> In those first few days when it was so darned hard, to be very honest, a few times I thought then that, gosh, it certainly would be nice if there had been a son or so to turn to, to feel that you weren't completely alone. But that comes of your weakness and loneliness of the moment. Eventually, naturally, you get back in stride and you're the master of your ship again, and things go on.
>
> Marge, age 76

Marge's feelings were temporary; she gathered strength and found needed solace in female friendships. She recovered from her loss by modeling herself after her favorite aunt who was widowed before her. And she thought beyond her aunt, to "all the millions of widows all over this world and forever backwards, and I thought, 'why, they all managed and you can too.'"

Later on in the interview I asked Marge if she felt regrets about the way her life had gone. She answered, "Well, it doesn't have to do with children." Clearly, she regretted the fact that her husband died young. And because of the Depression, she had to change her sights from going to college and writing "the world's greatest novel" to entering business to make her way.

For another woman the loss of her younger brother led to a brief reconsideration of her reproductive preference and guilt feelings over her abortion at the age of thirty-five. Although she was at an age when she still had the option to attempt pregnancy when her brother died, her "passing thoughts" proved to be a fleeting reaction to the loss of an important bond. When I asked Louise if she experienced any lingering conflict around the abortion and remaining childless she answered:

> No, it really hasn't been a conflict. I mean, I'm a normal person, and from time to time, especially when my brother was killed a couple of years ago, and he didn't have any children, I thought, "oh I feel guilty, you know, I should have had a child" or da da da. And I could have. But I mean I didn't . . . I thought about it. I thought there is no reason to have a child. I mean, it is for some people but it wouldn't be for me. And there were other points when I felt a little bit of pressure or kind of like, "oh, it might be nice." But I have to be honest, I just was never really interested in it.
>
> Louise, age 43

For still another woman, Gloria, feelings of self-doubt were related to her father's passing and her mother's present illness. She explained how her normally serene relationship with her reproductive status became ruffled by her mother's stroke:

> I guess I think about it more than before, but that's because my mother recently had a stroke and because she has such a large family. If you could say that someone can be happy with a stroke and they're

totally immobile and they can't talk, then my mother would be one of them because she's got her children taking care of her. There are so many of us and we're taking care of her. She's living at home, she gets pampered and loved, but that's because there were eight of us and two grandchildren that she helped raise who treat her like a mother. And I think, "My God, if something like that happens to me, it's a nursing home for me." Because there is nobody. But then that's selfish isn't it, to think about having children so that they can take care of you when you are old (laughing).

Gloria, age 43

For women who were caring for an ill or aging parent at the time of the interview, they couldn't help but wonder, as Elaine said it, "and who will do this for me?" Another woman, Helene, quipped that although she has experienced nothing at all resembling regret, she might have regrets "if I'm alone in the nursing home and other people are getting visitors and I'm not."

For numerous women, moments of questioning their childless practice were tied to concerns about their futures. One of the questions I asked women was, "If my research is published as a book, would you be interested in reading it?" One woman said, jokingly, she would turn right to the discussions of women in their sixties and seventies, "to see what's ahead for me, to see if I could find somebody like me who is happy." Women's concerns about aging without children are real enough, yet when they express their concerns, they are often incorrectly seen as regretful.

Another time that rumblings occurred for women was during transition times in their own lives, times when work became stale, times when they were going through periods of dissatisfaction or boredom or loneliness—those fallow times when life becomes drained of meaning and purpose. Linda, a woman seriously committed to remaining childless, was sterilized at age 30. She had this to say:

It really wasn't significant to me at all until probably, maybe a year ago. I think what happened is that I started to think about turning forty and about getting old and whatever that entails and about moving into a different part of my life. At that point I started wondering if

I did the right thing and I thought in recent times it was the right thing because I'm in the process of (pause) . . . I don't know what's going to happen with my consulting business, it's been a real upheaval for the last year or so and it's been real unpleasant for me. I've decided that maybe I'm going to walk away from it. I think it's time to focus on other things . . . When you sit still long enough you start thinking: "Gee, what do I want to do now? Well, gee, I can't have kids now, that's not going to occupy my time." In that context it's come up now. But it's never come up as a real sadness or never come up as something I've regretted. It's really only been something I've mused about.

Linda, age 40

And for Kay, second thoughts occurred when she felt lonely on a holiday that is associated with sociability and family gatherings:

Once made, the decision, I didn't have to think about it anymore. And I didn't have any second thoughts. There was only one time when I—not regret—but I felt sad that (pause). It was our last July 4th in Kennebunkport, so that must have been about four years ago. We were alone and we didn't have any company and there was no one around to celebrate with and we both felt very lonesome. And I thought at that time, "if I had had children we would have children around here. The kids would be teenagers by that time, but they would be in and out and there would be some contact with people." But that was the only time, just one day in all these years when I've kind of felt nostalgic about it. And it wasn't even a regret or it wasn't a change of heart but just the thought, "how would it have been different if I had had kids on this July 4th?" But that was the only time. And I haven't had that feeling since then.

Kay, age 46

Perhaps these thoughts and musings are not surprising when one considers the social meanings attached to children. For women especially, a child often represents an expectation of permanent security, a relationship that guarantees you will not be isolated or alone.[10] In periods of transition then, or of difficulty or boredom, it was not uncommon for some women to wonder if a child would "fix" their lives. The culture tells women that if they are not a mother they are missing out. At those points in women's lives

Symbolic Politics II

when they were missing something, it's not surprising that they sometimes wondered if a child would correct whatever problem they experienced. Maybe the grass is greener for mothers? Of course mothers have lonely times as well.

Sometimes women connected their rumblings directly to age transitions, but not to the final ticks of the biological clock as is often assumed. In fact, every woman except one who participated in this study rejected such a notion. Only one woman reported experiencing the "now or never" feelings or an emerging desire to reproduce at the last minute. Such sentiments may be more characteristic of late-timing mothers.

However, a sense of oneself as permanently childless did develop for some women *after* they lost the option to reproduce. As one woman said, "I never thought of myself as someone who would never have children." And for another woman, saying "I've not had children rather than I'm not having children" aroused feelings of wistfulness.

At these times when their childless state surfaced, women reported curiosity about the road not taken. Women wondered what their children might have looked like and they wondered what kind of parents they would have been. "I think I would have been a good parent and I never got to test it out." One woman was sorry that she would never have the experience of nursing a baby. In none of these cases was the curiosity or questioning strong enough to reverse their ongoing practice of childlessness, if indeed it wasn't too late:

> The part that I find sad is, I think we would have been good parents. We obviously could provide a comfortable life for a child. I think we would have had something to offer as parents. But, not to the point of being willing to offer it.
>
> Lee Bishop, age 45

Another woman mentioned being wistful about losing "a normal female experience that I will never have." Still another woman spoke of mourning the loss, not of a child, "but of the *option* we have enjoyed. It's a closing of a chapter, saying okay, this is our life.

There is no going back." In a sense then, the full force of remaining childless is not felt by some women until midlife when the practice becomes finalized. Being a mother is given such a place of importance in this culture that some women found it hard when the option was gone forever: "It's damn difficult to slam that door shut once and for all."

A couple of women spoke knowingly about how they avoided rumblings by unrealistically refusing to close the door. The narrators "kept choice alive" by using adoption or foster care as back-up positions. In the context of talking about her sterilization decision, Linda told this story:

> We decided that, well, if we were not going to have kids of our own, we could always adopt. It was nothing more than a back-up position. I mean, it's nothing more than swaying. "I'm never going to have a kid period" is real hard to say to people, to do, to cut that off. So you do what you do, you leave that open and say, "Well, we can always adopt if we want a kid."
>
> Linda, age 40

Beth spoke of years when she could say unequivocally, "I will not have children. I will never conceive." Yet she would not say, "I won't bring children into my home to raise them." Even though she knows it will not happen, she treats children as an ongoing possibility:

> Maybe once in the last year I said to Steve, "What would you think about, in the future, like when I finish my program, doing foster care for infants?" And then we both laughed. Like sure, count on it. That to me is the same romantic notion of having a baby. That's the part of me that just *loves* babies, and children too.
>
> Beth, age 44

A number of women connected their passing thoughts to historical transitions. My interviews were conducted during the late 1980s and early 1990s, a period of backlash against feminist gains during previous decades. Maternalism was in resurgence. Some women reported *feeling* their childlessness in a way they hadn't a decade earlier. One woman stated she feels "more political about it, more different because of it" now. Remember Elaine's words at the beginning of the introductory chapter: "Why aren't younger women thinking about *not* having children? Why aren't I the hero?" she asks herself. "My choice is valid and it's never been discovered."

Maria's needs for intimacy and community were met in the days of her undaunting activism. She had deep ties to feminist friends and a community seeking political solutions to personal problems. Her rumblings about the childless state appear in the context of a loss of community, of the historical shift away from public to personal life:

> I still go to various meetings and things but I feel like there is not the same emotional buoying effect I used to get from working on projects with some folks. Now we all seem to be into respective careers . . . the political commitment is no longer one that seems productive. The odds are just too overwhelming. So we are looking maybe to some kind of individual solution.
>
> Maria, age 43

Lastly, some women experienced rumblings when they were around children. As I discuss in some detail in the next chapter, many women enjoyed the company of children and contributed to their lives in significant ways. Most women realized that children are a source of unique pleasures as well as a lot of work and responsibility. One woman talked about having "twinges" sometimes when she's around her sister's children—they add fun to her life.

Ellen recognizes that "there's a great deal of joy that can come from having wonderful children. When my best friend has her kid's Sweet Sixteen party, I can get a great deal of joy out of seeing this one little girl, who used to be ten and now is sixteen and is on her way to being a fully formed person. You can get some level of joy. It's not the same as having your own."

Claire said it this way: "I think we would have had a hell of a good time with a kid . . . It's not a lack that I feel, it's something that would have been fun to do." For Margaret, the feeling is not, "Oh, we've passed this thing up. But you know, kids are kind of neat, it might have been fun. It's more like what would be really nice is to live in an extended situation with other people where we could be like an aunt and uncle, so we could do things with kids, you know."

Women recognized the pleasures that come with children but that did not mean they regretted being childless. They didn't. But some recognized that they incurred losses by remaining childless. "Perhaps if you could just skip the middle step and go right to the grandchildren, I would have liked that . . . I mean, grandchildren seem to be the best part of the whole deal when you look at it objectively." Another woman described her sense of loss as "a loss with a small 'l'." One participant said that when she's around happy children and wonders if she should have had a child, her thoughts are momentary—"then all the reality shoots back."

Although nearly all the women I interviewed did not identify themselves as regretful *now*, several did wonder if they would feel regret in the future. Rhonda, at age 48, states: "I'd like to know whether (the decision) comes back to haunt at a later date. Is there a period of life that I haven't reached yet where it is going to come back and I'm going to be sorry about the decision? If somebody has any insights into that, it would be interesting to know."

Research reported by Alexander, Rubinstein, Goodman, and Luborsky, although perhaps limited in applicability to my self-defined intentionally childless population, does offer important insights into the issue of later life regrets.[11] Exploring the cultural context of regret, Alexander et al. interviewed ninety childless women over the age of sixty, the majority of whom were European–American (ten percent were African–American), and most of whom were involuntarily childless (never–married women, late–married women, women with health and fertility problems). The authors conclude that women's regrets late in life were "shaped and formed in the context of a culture that defines womanhood predominantly through childbearing and that forces women to evaluate themselves continually against the pressure of this cultural prescription."[12]

These researchers found that women reported regretful feelings increasing in intensity with age. Their feelings of incompleteness and lack of fulfillment were directly tied to their acceptance of maternalist ideology. The comment of one woman illustrates the point: "I think that's why women are here, partly, to have families and all . . . I really think that's what the female is designed for and that she, I really think your life isn't complete."[13]

Regretful feelings were also usually context-dependent and therefore not constant. Especially in relationships with mothering women who often talked about children and grandchildren, childless women felt like outsiders, which increased feeling regretful. Further, and not surprisingly, women missed having children at a time in life when they felt more vulnerable and dependent since they believed children were morally obligated to provide care.

Like my mostly younger sample, Alexander et al.'s older group of women resisted as well as embraced pejorative social definitions of childlessness. Regrets coexisted with cultural criticism in the speech of not–mothers. Indeed, some women voiced no regrets, only criticism of societal stereotyping. Whether or not women defined themselves as regretful, in later life childless women may feel extra pressure to justify their lives as meaningful. In short, the personal is political; childless women's rumblings are not independent of cultural context.

To summarize, it is not surprising that the majority of not–mothers I spoke with are challenged by moments or periods of internal questioning related to their childless state, no matter how committed they were to that state. Participants experienced rumblings and engaged in speculations about what might have been if they had had children. Rumblings were not considered problematic by most, but rather just temporary musings that happen from time to time depending on circumstances. Family transitions, age, and social context were related to consciousness of childless status. A settled issue becomes temporarily unsettling. Second thoughts took place within the larger context of ongoing reinforcement of childlessness. Weak moments were most often associated with a mild emotional tone, like wistfulness, or a feeling of generalized anxiety about the future. Only occasionally were such rumblings described as painful. For most, they just seemed to be a part of the experience of remaining a not–mothering woman. Those women who had greater discomfort with their status had to come to terms with their internalized beliefs about childless women and their idealized fantasies about motherhood.

Research on the experiences of women who are mothers reveals that this group experiences its own moments of doubt. Indeed, in *The Motherhood Report,* authors Genevie and Margolies found that the majority of the 1,100 mothers they interviewed were ambivalent about their mothering role. And in the last couple of years, feminists who are mothers have begun to speak out against maternalism. In an article in *Off Our Backs,* "Am I the Only Woman Who Regrets Having Children?" the author laments:

> With Mother's Day having just passed I find myself feeling, once again, frustrated, guilty and depressed about being a mother. All around I am being told how wonderful motherhood is and how it is the loftiest realm a woman could ever hope to occupy. At the very worst it is seen as being "challenging," but nothing ever suggests that maybe, just maybe, some women do not like being mothers.[14]

But this kind of reflection is not part of the common public discourse about mothering, and when it appears, it is sensationalized. The implicit suggestion is that not–mothers think (regretfully) about children but mothers are not bothered by losses incurred by their choices. Thus discourses that project regret onto childless women make motherhood a necessary route to comfort and satisfaction and at the same time lay claim to the inner lives of childless women.

Final Thoughts on Symbolic Politics

Conceptual distinctions rooted in reproductive difference create an interdependent hierarchy among women. Maternalist ideology depends on the depreciation of not–mothers to discipline women's desires and behaviors in the direction of motherhood. Women who refuse this direction (or cannot achieve mothering status) are symbolically censured and may find themselves struggling with internalized negative images.

When symbolic distinctions are blurred, mechanisms come into play to reinstate them.[15] Because maternalist thinking is completely braided with and hidden in everyday discourses that are accepted without question, the fact that this thought pattern is actively generated by the dominant cultural group *because it is consistent with the dominant group's interests* is forgotten. Maternalism is part of the dominant belief system and is comprised of myths that do not offer an accurate description of women's lives.[16]

Even though the real boundaries of gender have changed, the symbolic boundaries remain. "Motherhood" remains a powerful signifier of women's normality and superior caring abilities. Negative representations of childlessness, combined with a largely implicit positive view of motherhood, disguise the fact that both not–mothers and mothers experience costs and benefits related to reproductive status. If mothers and not–mothers were equally privileged in the symbolic life of the culture, images of the nuclear family would become less seductive, and what are now fearful images of living outside the norm would become more attractive. Thus patriarchal power would lose an important reinforcer.

6

"The contrast between their lives and your life puts a wedge between your friendship"
THE SOCIAL WORLD OF CHILDLESS WOMEN

All women may currently occupy the position "woman" . . . but they do not occupy it in the same way.

—Mary Poovey[1]

MANY continuing aspects of social life are organized on the assumption that people live in families—families defined as parents and children. When a woman in a long-term, live-in heterosexual union remains childless, her personal arrangements contradict societal assumptions, recasting expected social relations. A unique set of pleasures and tensions is experienced.

Some of the relationship repercussions of childlessness were described in my discussion of the ongoing explanatory work in which women engage. In this chapter I focus directly upon women's affiliations with their partners, with children, and with their friends, especially those who are mothers. As I hope to show, not having children of one's own has paradoxical consequences for one's social relations.

When women summarized what remaining without children had meant for their lives, they most often used the word "freedom." Spaces away from the emotional and time demands of others, and time for chosen pursuits were clear benefits. But as I explore in the closing section of this chapter, this freedom was not without complications.

The Couple Nest: Power and Vulnerability

Most of the women in my sample both resisted and embraced marriage. By not complying with one of the central mandates of marriage—reproduction—they created an alternative form of nuclear family life to meet their sexual, emotional, and material needs. This alternative structure was understood to involve both compensations and perils.

Whether participants negotiated to minimize inequality before agreeing to marriage, or whether "an equal kind of thing" evolved over time, woman after woman reported a relationship based on "supportive love and deep friendship."[2] In one woman's words, "All of who Walter is is of assistance to me, as I know that I am to him. If anything, I can do more of what I want to do, being in this relationship, than if I were alone." For another woman, "Friendship with Roger is extremely important. When everything else, and everything else can go strange all at one time, what I have here is the thing that I use as my resource." Four of the women did not consent to formal marriage. But these women in common law relationships also expressed pleasure in their partnerships. Maria said, "I love not being married . . . We have real separate lives and a real close friendship."

In short, the experiences and interpretations of not–mothers provide an optimistic view of the possibilities for mutual love and shared power in heterosexual relationships. Contrary to popular ideas about differing psychological orientations between the sexes making intimacy nearly impossible, the reports of this group suggest that some of the relational gaps between men and women are structural in origin rather than psychologically fixed.

The spacious closeness that most of the women experienced was directly related to the rejection of traditional gender roles of wife and mother. Indeed, in remarkably consistent fashion, most women interviewed refused identification with the term "wife," which connoted to them a subordinate social role:

(I think of myself) as a partner rather than a wife. Wife conjures up a stereotype that I don't feel I am. I'm a lousy wife. I guess what is very popular and common now was not the case when John and I were married. We were both finishing up our graduate degrees. And we shared chores because we had to do them catch-as-catch-can. So my husband has never been doted upon. He had been single for some time. He knew how to take care of himself. I don't pack his clothes when we go away. So I'm not a serving person. It's a shared thing . . . So my image of what I was brought up to be, just as probably you were, was that a wife does all of these things, the laundry and the shopping and the cooking and the cleaning. And I don't do all those things. So I don't identify as a wife . . . But certainly we both feel we're each other's best friends. And so partner is a better word for me. Nothing tagged to that.

Carole, age 55

I don't think of myself as a wife. Not at all. I have a very close relationship with my husband. We work together on many, many projects. We are together a lot in the week, more so than most people, have lots of the same interests and values and yet I don't consider myself a wife. It's just not part of my thinking.

Elizabeth, age 48

I think of myself as a person who can make long and lasting friendships with people and be a good friend. And I think of Doug as a kind of special case of that . . . I think we're really a very good complement. I think I do a lot of good things for him and he's very good for me. We have a lot of intellectual interests and a lot of political interests, and we just talk and talk and we never get bored with each other. And it's always fun to be around each other.

Margaret, age 41

I'm a wife although I always find it odd to call myself that somehow because I don't feel a husband-wife relationship with my significant other. We're just such good friends that it really does feel odd to say, "oh yes, I guess I am his wife, I guess he is my husband." It's more like my buddy. I just realize as you are saying to me to describe yourself that I rarely think of myself as wife. As attached to him, yes. That's interesting. I wonder if that has something to do with not having kids. I wonder if women who don't have children more often don't think of themselves as wives, that role kind of slips away somewhere. That's interesting.

Claire, age 45

Economic autonomy was clearly related to experiences of equality. One woman mentioned only acting like a wife when she lost her own income. Deena, a psychiatrist married to an auto worker, was the high wage earner in her family until she decided to go back to school for further specialized training. She poignantly expressed the psychic costs of not earning an income:

> I went back to school and dropped everything but continued to maintain my office and pay that rent and stuff. I was way in the hole. That was an interesting change. Because my husband was obviously making a lot more than I was. It was interesting in terms of what I felt I had to do. You talk about being a wife. That's when I started doing all the washing. I felt I had to do everything because I wasn't bringing in the money I used to. We still split expenses. I had enough to maintain my share. But I would weasel out of things. Like if we used to go out to eat we would always split everything in half and I'd weasel free dinners. So for that I thought I had to do these other things, all the wash, the house, everything.
>
> Deena, age 49

Many of the narrators linked maximizing intimacy and equalizing power in their marriage relationship to remaining childless and thus avoiding subordinating structural arrangements that mothers have a difficult time escaping. One need only review the earlier chapter on choice to see that women's avoidance of motherhood was braided with their desires for roomy relationships with partners and shared authority.

Women also perceived remaining childless as a way to bypass a deep level of interpersonal conflict they believed parents experienced. They believed their relationships were closer and more intense than those found in marriages with children because of a greater commitment of emotional and real time which could be devoted to the relationship:

> I think our relationship is built upon being good friends and being supportive of each other's careers. And I think if we had children, just as we're very different types of people in many, many ways, I think those differences would be highlighted if we had children. We have dogs and they have no dog obedience training whatsoever. That's

Ralph. I'm embarrassed by that. If those were my children I would want them to behave better. It's easy to say the dogs are his, but if we had children it wouldn't be so easy to do.

Linda, age 40

My sense is that marriages are frayed, not strengthened with children. I think that one can relax in one's relationship in a way that having kids makes hard, having to make sure that somebody's doing this, that, and the other thing, and putting up with the craziness and the stress that goes on. And I don't see those marriages getting unfrayed. I see these things as permanent distances. I know it's alleged to be a cementing force but I've only seen it go the other way.

Jo, age 43

I think that sometimes, actually, you're closer because you depend on each other more. Of course, it eliminates a lot of strife too, because from what I see, mothers and fathers have so many problems some-times with these children which we don't have . . . They're so wrapped up in the activities of their children. This way we're wrapped up in each other's activities, more or less. Although we each go our own way, which is good. We're not too dependent on each other that way.

Cara, age 78

I hesitate to say this because it sounds really selfish, but I see that so many (mothers) miss having fun in their marriages. I don't believe in having romance in my marriage, I believe in having fun. Because I don't know what romance is. Romance, to me, is candlelight and wine and stuff like that. Fun encompasses it all. It's that, it's being able to take time for each other, it's caring, and I see a lot of women missing that. Never really getting to know their husbands. I see them as resentful because of what they have to give, the amount of time they have to give to their children. I see some of them burning the candle at both ends, doing the job thing and the children and family thing. And missing enjoying any of it.

Rhonda, age 46

Importantly, the women speaking above are not suggesting that they found an "exceptional man" or that they themselves embody personal characteristics that mothers lack. Rather, these women attribute the differences they identify to structural conditions. Just as women felt that they could not "do both" motherhood and independent work without excessive costs they were unwilling to pay, so they felt they could not "do both" motherhood and have the pleasurable and equitable relationship with their partner that they valued.

Other researchers have also found this reported pleasure in marriage among childless women. After reviewing the social science literature, Susan S. Lang reported that women without children are generally happier with their marriages than are mothers. Married mothers, for the most part, are under more financial pressure, and they've got more chores and less time and less help from husbands.[3] Elaine Campbell found that the term "partnership" appeared frequently in her discussions with 78 childless couples in a large Scottish city. She found a strong emphasis placed on sharing, companionship, friendship, comfort, and affection among her sample.

Such closeness might become too much of a good thing. Although no woman in my sample reported an uncomfortable intensity in her marital relationship, some childless women do. In her memoir, Molly Haskell writes: "Childless couples often become this way: so close you can't see air between them. The intensity can be suffocating but it happens gradually and pleasurably, like anesthesia or like climbing at high altitude, so that in your euphoria you don't even realize you're taking in less oxygen than the normal person." According to her husband, Andrew Sarris, the lack of children in their marriage is more a symptom than the cause of the intensity of the relationship.[4]

Campbell points out that even though a pattern of marital harmony among the childless emerges, remaining without children is no guarantee of stress-free relationships. In my sample, women overall were remarkably pleased with their relationships. They were also midlife and older and in long-term relationships. Earlier stresses had been successfully negotiated and relationships were stable and comfortable. It is also worth remarking that seven women were in their second marriages. If they had been interviewed when they were younger childless women in their first marriages, the data would indeed look different. My point is that age may be an important variable in the overall pleasure women took in their partnerships.

In conclusion, some structural attributes of childless marriages appear to facilitate egalitarian partnerships in the sample of women I interviewed. Whether marriages without children are *generally* more egalitarian than marriages with children is a question worth future research. According to Diane Ehrensaft, who studied co-parenting partners, parenthood itself can be a pathway to more egalitarianism in a couple relationship.[5] But as Ann Oakley soberly contends: ". . . It is first-time motherhood which forces women to confront the real feminine dilemma. Before that, and as I had done in my early housewife–undergraduate days, you can pretend you're equal. Once there's a baby to care for, you can't."[6]

These women chose and preferred this particular family structure, but most of them, whatever their age, experienced anxiety about the future given their location half-in and half-out of a nuclear family arrangement. Children, especially daughters and daughters-in-law, provide substantial emotional and material support to their aging parents. Diana Gittins argues that the "care of the elderly in contemporary society is carried out more by families than it was in the past; labels such as 'community care' are only a thin disguise for the reality of care by female kin."[7] The fact that children can be a kind of social insurance, combined with the fact that women are much more likely to live longer than their male partners, creates real world problems for not–mothers. They face a shortage of the labor power that children provide.

Most narrators were aware of this social reality. Some registered concern about this labor shortage while others shunned all thoughts of later life dependency. Linda poignantly recognized, "I will lack an advocate." Elaine was concerned that "there will be no one who will be taking care of me because I'm me." "It's me against the world" was Cara's response. "*I* will be taking care of me" was how Marge said it. When I asked Ann on whom she might depend in the future, if need be, she responded, "Well, I am my own support system. If I can't rely on me, I certainly can't rely on somebody else." Edith thinks, "I will always be able to take care of myself, I mean, emotionally, financially, so I'm just not concerned about it. I plan to be in very good health and I plan to be able to take care of myself. It's just that simple. I have nobody to fall back on, it's me."

Childless women may indeed be at a greater risk of isolation in later life than mothers, given their existence within a truncated nuclear family form. With advancing age, husbands and wives come to depend very heavily upon each other to meet social, psychic, and physical needs. Partners tend to rely upon each other exclusively. As Marge phrased it earlier, "we were each other's world." For the handful of later life participants, a certain degree of isolation was indeed an issue. Although neither Cara (age 78) nor Susan (age 74) were widowed, Cara thought having the support of children at this stage in life would "make things easier." And Susan stated, "we have nobody." Marge's circumstance was somewhat different. Although she is also in her seventies, she was widowed young. With a long experience as a single woman she built a supportive network of family and friends. Still, many of her friends are around her own age and it is not clear who will end up providing needed assistance to whom.

Research suggests that childless married women are more vulnerable to isolation than never–married childless women. Barbara Levy Simon reports that in middle and late middle age, never–married women "solidified and deepened their friendships and involved their closest friends in planning for life after retirement."[8] And, not surprisingly, their friends were other women. Although largely invisible, alternative support networks are utilized by never–married women who live on the margins of the nuclear family form. By contrast, the married women I interviewed made their plans with their husbands, often separated from even the closest of friends.

Yet childless married women can and do develop durable interdependent ties beyond the couple. The minority of participants who were not concerned about being old without "an advocate" were building friendship webs that extended well beyond their marriages. They thus developed a different assumption than the majority. Sara is an example of a woman who has many intimates as well as "an ongoing belief that I will always be connected to people in a vital way." Research on later life families suggests that, although older childless individuals are more likely to live alone and be more socially isolated than older persons with children, they are not lonelier and are as likely to have someone in whom to confide. Social isolation becomes problematic when the health of the childless elder declines.[9]

Women's attitudes and practices are important; so is social policy. It appears that the rewards and risks of living in the couple nest are interrelated, given the ideology and structural organization of the nuclear family. If families were less privatized and more socially supported, perhaps women who chose to enter into marriages would be freer to choose whether to have children. Biological children would be less necessary for social insurance and enduring relationship with nonbiological children would be more possible. The rewards of childlessness might then outweigh real present and future risks.

Children: Solidarity and Distances

It is commonly assumed that women who remain childless do not like children, have no relationships with children, and are not competent to meet children's needs. This was far from the case among the women I met. Nearly one half of the participants had worked or were working directly with children or were involved in work that directly benefitted children. Three-quarters of the sample spoke of friendships they had with a particular child or children, most often relatives or children of good friends. The remaining seven women described themselves as either not child-oriented or as uncomfortable around children.

In general, the women I spoke with expressed solidarity with the needs of younger people. As demonstrated in a previous chapter, their respect for children's needs in some cases was related to the decision to remain childless, given competing commitments. As one woman expressed it, she never had a strong pull towards motherhood but always experienced a strong pull towards children. Work with or for children encompassed both paid work and volunteer and activist commitments. Several women worked, or had worked in the past, as child educators. "My whole gig is working with kids in music . . . I love kids." Several worked with children as therapists. Others worked in behalf of children as activists or as academics. For example, one woman created a slide show on child sexual abuse that has been shown internationally. Another participant authored a book on childhood language problems and interventions. Still another touched children's lives every day as a feminist-oriented trial lawyer specializing in custody disputes. One woman, who held a powerful position in the armed services, taught in the public schools when she retired. Looking back, it was the teaching that meant more to her than her prestigious military career:

> I'd say that the teaching part has been the most satisfying part because of the contacts with children, because of the opportunity to remove from many kids fears about learning, fears about themselves and opening doors of thought for them.
>
> Lee Henry, age 66

Sometimes women spoke of special friendships with their friends' children, bonds that satisfied a desire to nurture and relate to younger people. Lee Bishop mentioned, "I kind of share vicariously with friends' children that I'm very close to and I watch them develop. The evolution of this little creature to a person with their own thoughts." Such relationships with children allow childless women to comfortably join in nurturing activities without becoming mothers, and at the level of involvement that suits them.[10] Ellen asserted, "I've chosen to be Auntie Mame rather than any type of full-time parent."

Women spoke of special friendships with nieces and nephews or children of friends that were often close and intense, and participants saw themselves as making real contributions to their growth and welfare:

> Lucky for me that I was not one of those with a strong need to (become) a mother because if I had it would be real difficult. I think part of the reason I don't have a strong need to become a mother is because . . . I come from such a huge family and because I have a

niece and a nephew. If I didn't have those two kids that I almost see as my children, if I weren't in the work that I'm in where I can do the mothering types of things, then I don't know that I would be as comfortable with myself as I am.

See, I mold lives every day in my work. My patients, I heal their lives. Some patients of mine have told me: "You know you're my honorary mother." I've molded the lives of (my niece and nephew). I feel very strongly that the reason one of them is in a doctoral program is because of my influence and she's told me that. "I wouldn't be in graduate school if it weren't that from the time I was little you used to tell me, you've got to go to school, you've got to go to school."

So I have had that mothering, not in the traditional way, but I have that . . . There are some people who don't want to be mothers and that's okay. And there's some people who want to be mothers in a different way, and that's me and that's okay. I don't think you have to be a traditional mother in order to be successful and happy.

Gloria, age 43

Another woman described her friend's child, Megan, as being "'my special person' in that family." She described to me her role as Megan's advocate at the birth of Megan's brother:

I sent for and got Megan right away. Megan is my special person in that family. She was two and I brought her up and they had this nurse who was sort of taking care of the birth . . . And I got the nurse to allow me to bring Megan up and hold the baby. The baby had just been born and this little thing that couldn't do anything else closed his hand around this finger and I mean I was Megan's person and her advocate through all that and so she came to the hospital rather than waiting and not seeing her mother for a long time and waiting for the baby to come home and then all of a sudden having this thing there. I mean, she was really a part of it and that was real special.

Elaine, age 48

Elaine went on to describe herself and her husband as "sort of step-parents to a lot of kids. Where they stay over and we play the grandmother kind of role in that sense that ours is the nice place to come."

Other women spoke of their special connections to children. "If something happened to my sister, would I take her twelve year old? In a second. I'd fight tooth and nail." And again, "My nieces and nephews, several of them, I would be delighted to have them come live with us." And again, "Even now I've become a parent with other children. When they have problems they call me."

Women generally characterized the relationships they developed with children as friendships, suggesting a less hierarchical arrangement than "parent-child" demands. One woman's nephews and nieces commented to her that she didn't take "the mother stance." This was related to not having to take the role of disciplinarian or feel a "final responsibility" for the child. The friendships, then, tended to be rather conflict-free sources of pleasure and fun and unconditional support.

Two women who had relationships with children did not have such happy stories. And several others described themselves as either not child-oriented or as uncomfortable around young people. One woman, whose emotionally troubled eight year old step-son lived with her for a period of a year, had an agonizing time. Finally, she laid it on the line with her husband: "Look either he goes or I go:"

> It was a *horrible* year for all of us. I knew almost from the beginning I had made a mistake. I couldn't handle this child. And my husband was going back to New York once a month for family reasons. So he was out of town three to five days a month and I had this child by myself. And I wasn't getting the emotional support from him that I needed. He did not participate in taking care of this child with me like I thought he should be. And so I felt very alone with this . . . And then by the end of the twelfth month I said either he goes or I go. And that took a lot of guts to say that. And so he went.
>
> Kay, age 46

Another woman spoke of her husband's daughter as "a miserable little creature." And one woman spoke of her nieces and nephews as "yukky." Another woman had no love lost for her brother's son: "He's got 'white trash' embroidered on his vest—that's my nephew!" A minority of women, then, voiced their preference to keep children at a distance. Sometimes a particular child was involved, sometimes women just did not appreciate being in the company of children.

Not all women who wanted children in their lives had easy access to children. One woman mentioned her frustration at wanting to participate in the lives of children but not finding any available. She had great fondness for her nieces and nephews but they lived thousands of miles away. And the children of friends were very involved with their own biological families. "They have their own Mommies and Daddies and Aunts and Uncles." Another woman felt equally frustrated by how hard it is to develop deep and enduring relationships with children without "owning" them.

When women did become honorary aunts or godmothers, when they developed close relationships with the children outside their own family networks, they recognized that these would not necessarily be long-standing relationships. Whereas social norms and laws define the reciprocal nature of the parent–child bond, there are no societal expectations of mutual support across the life course between adults and children not so formally related. Maria summarizes the contradictions of her relationships with children in the following way:

> In some ways it is the best of both possible worlds because it's like being a granny. You go bowling with the children when you want them but they are not under foot when you don't want them there. Of course, the down side is that they are not your children. They are not your special ones that you are raising so they aren't going to be there when you are needing them. They have their own Mommy and Daddy to look after when they are older.
>
> Maria, age 43

The women in my sample who were retired did not describe close friendships with young children. Their nieces and nephews and children of friends were now adults. One woman in her late seventies lived in a retirement home which was age segregated. Another woman lived in her own home and described her enjoyment of seeing children on a daily basis. She describes not close friendships but a more detached appreciation:

> There's a young couple who live next door to me here, and I've known them since she bought the house first and next thing I knew

she had a friend living there, and then next thing I knew they were married, and then the next thing I knew they had two children. And it's just been like a little story book that I've been watching. And I'm very well acquainted with both of them and their children, and we're very fond of each other and all. And so I don't feel deprived in any way. But I mean it's not anything I ever yearn for, for myself. But I have enjoyed watching those little kids grow up. I guess they are only five and four years old now. And I live across the street from an elementary school, and it happens to be that the kindergarten is located in the end of the building which faces my home. I watch that little parade in the morning when I have breakfast. I fix my breakfast on a tray and take it in the living room and watch TV and the morning news while I have breakfast. But out of the corner of my eye I'm aware of that little parade across the street and all their little bright colored snowsuits and going up to the school. It's just like a little picture, like a little Grandma Moses painting. And so if you see what I mean, I'm not somebody who is down on children. But I just don't feel that need myself.

Marge, age 76

Margaret, whose life work is societal transformation, summed up how she hopes remaining childless will assist her in contributing to the welfare of all children:

I hope that since I haven't had children and I haven't really had to put personal activities on hold because I was taking care of children and keeping things together for us as a little social unit and just spending all my time taking care of other people and that I've been able to develop myself more as an individual and as a political person, I hope that I will be able to do other kinds of things, other kinds of nurturing things . . . I have hopes that my political work could be something that is life-affirming in another sense than having children. That it would be about human beings and human values and people having good lives in a maybe more abstract, but still connected way. I mean, I still think that if I'm very successful, I'll be able to do something for kids, to help make the world into a more human world.

Margaret, age 41

It is inaccurate to assume that because a woman is not a biological or adoptive mother, she is disinterested in children or does not engage in raising children. Her participation in and contribution to the lives of younger people often remain invisible and unacknowledged. Writers and theorists such as Patricia Hill Collins, bell hooks, and Adrienne Rich have addressed this issue. Collins speaks of the collaborative nature of nurturing and childrearing among African–American women and uses words such as "bloodmothers," "other–mothers," and "community other–mothers."[11] Collins makes the point that the nuclear heterosexual family is neither natural nor universally preferred. She also flags a way of blurring the boundaries between the exclusive categories "mother" and "childless." The potential problem here is turning all women into some-kind-of-mother, a concern I return to in the concluding chapter.

Berenice Fisher and others suggest the concept of a mothering continuum, a thought model originating with Adrienne Rich. This view recognizes that the either/or distinction between mothers and childless women, tied as it is to the white, middle-class ideal, harms all women. I like Fisher's summary:

> Rich's thinking suggests that we can view mothering and childlessness on a continuum, a continuum based on our actual emotional and physical relation to children. Women might be located anywhere along that continuum, rather than being assigned to either category of mother or that of childless woman.
>
> I like this notion of a mothering continuum because it might enable a variety of women—childless women, would-be mothers, active mothers, mothers with grown children—to talk together about the meaning of children in our lives.[12]

Fisher goes on to say that such a continuum allows room for women who are very involved with children as well as women who prefer to avoid children "without passing judgement on either way of living. The continuum image also leaves room for mothers who do not want to spend much time with children and for men who do."[13]

Given the political importance of language in constructing reality, I prefer to follow the lead of bell hooks, who speaks about childrearing rather than mothering. A childrearing continuum recognizes the

ork of women who are not bloodmothers. Childrearers
re include teachers, social workers, therapists, child care
bysitters, and so on. Childrearers do not have to be par-
d such care providers do not have to be women. bell
hooks aks persuasively about the limits of the white, middle-
class co-parenting model. Many women are not in a position to
share daily childraising activities with a male partner. hooks argues
that there is a growing need for community-based child care that
brings children into relationships with male childrearers "so they
will not grow to maturity thinking women are the only group who
do or should do childrearing."[14]

Childrearing may best be understood as a continuum, but in a
materialistic and consumer society childless women do lack something central: the child as commodity. Philosopher and ethicist
Christine Overall states that children are not valued for their own
sake, but as a type of consumer good.[15] She explains:

> If children are like a commodity, then, for those who desire that com-
> modity (regardless of how the desire has been acquired), it will be
> important to obtain one's *own*. It is not enough to appreciate and
> enjoy children for their own sake; one must come to *possess* one or
> more. This idea is apparent in the passage by Robert Edwards quoted
> earlier. He refers to couples who had suffered "years of childlessness."
> He is not suggesting, of course, that these people did not have a
> chance to know children, to interact with them, work or play with
> them, teach them, or care for them. For all we know, the couples
> involved could include child care workers or teachers, pediatricians or
> playground supervisors, librarians or camp counselors, all of whom
> have ample opportunity to be with children. Or they might be none
> of these. The point is that it does not matter. What is important is not
> being with children but having them, having one's own. Children are
> a type of property.[16]

And having one's own does change one's social location and relationships, just as not having one affects relationships.

Women do not commonly think in terms of such abstract categories as "childrearing." Traditional and contemporary ideas about
"having" children, coupled with social conditions under which

women must rear them, contribute to divisions between mothers and childless women, a key relationship problem to which I now turn.

Friendship Wedges

. . . when the parents are raising their children they are not too available and they are so tied up with the childrearing that it's almost like the contrast between their lives and your life puts a wedge between your friendship.

Maria, age 43

In her article, "Motherhood and Friendship," Susan Shapiro, writing as a new mother, identifies unexpected tensions in her relationships with childless friends.[17] Her friends without children resented the fact that she was less available to the friendship; she in turn felt their loss of support and understanding. Another problem was diverging interests. According to Shapiro, many childless women are bored with the details of a child's daily life at the same time that mothers often find their children "the most fascinating subject in the universe and . . . could talk about them forever."[18] Both these wedges—lack of availability and deviating interests—appeared in my conversations with participants. In addition, emotional distances occurred when narrators felt their competency to contribute to children's lives questioned.

Women sometimes felt left out and left behind when friends became mothers. When I asked one woman if she had any friends who were mothers she answered:

I would say no. Martha I teach with. When we first came here I think Martha and I were close, and we talk and we're friends, but we're not close and that really happened around the time when she had kids. Her whole life was those kids, which is fine, but I quite frankly get bored with it, and it's not my life. We had a parting of the ways and she got in with a group of mothers and I just got sick of looking at the pictures. I wasn't real patient . . . My friends are people like Ann and Lynn. Then the people in Boston that I'm closest to don't have kids.

Linda, age 40

Numerous women reported that once-close friendships gradually declined as the time, activities, and interests of their friends turned toward mothering:

> All of a sudden somebody would have a baby. And they would talk about having a bowel movement a day, or playing in the sand, or whatever. And I'd think, "Gee, here we were involved in the war movement together or feminism or whatever we were involved with—how has this taken precedence over that?" And then the gap would occur and you wouldn't see them . . .
>
> Cathy, age 45

Some women spoke wistfully of losing the intimacy they once had with childless friends when those friends became mothers. Others spoke with resentment about friends who decided to become mothers. This was particularly true of women now in their forties, whose intentionally childless friends changed their minds in the closing "biological minutes." As Liz Heron points out, women who choose childlessness want to be supported in the rightness of their choice, just as mothers want to be supported in theirs.[19] In a period of resurgent interest in and idealization of motherhood, not–mothers experience dwindling validation for remaining childless. Increasing feelings of being on the outside often took a personalized turn:

> Everybody's, you know, talking about which day care center or that kind of thing that's not applicable to me. And so in that sense I don't have a lot to contribute to those conversations. But when conversations are about other things, I have a lot to contribute . . . in some ways . . . it is being an outsider. I guess I thought there would be more outsiders when I was in my twenties. You know, population zero was the big "in" thing. And I see a lot of people now having kids and I used to think, "Oh you turncoats, you made your decision and now you've changed your mind. You didn't have the guts to go through with it." Now I think, "Oh well, that's fine. They did what they needed to do."
>
> Barb, age 43

One participant recounted her feelings and reported on her commiserations with another childless woman about their friends who became late–timing mothers:

> Narrator: When women my age—this has actually been going on now ten years maybe—when women who I thought were not going to have kids had kids, women I was close to, I would really feel . . . it changes your relationship so drastically. I mean they normally have an attention span that long (gesturing) for everything else in the world. And I really have resented their decisions in some cases.
>
> Interviewer: What is the resentment?
>
> N: It's losing that friendship, not the friendship, but that relationship, that kind of closeness, that kind of attention.
>
> Jo, age 43

Jo continued in a humorous vain by saying that when she gets together with one of her friends "who is exactly like I am, we congratulate each other and say nasty things about our friends who (became mothers)":

> I: And when you congratulate each other, is it because you feel like you were able to resist and they weren't?
>
> N: Oh no. We are just smarter than they were. You know, that we really saw the whole thing clearly and they got sucked in by, you know, things they saw incorrectly (laughing).

Elaine enjoys an intense and ongoing relationship with her friend and her friend's children. A testimony to their closeness is the open contest that occurred over the meaning of Elaine's emotional pain and resentment when her friend decided to have a baby:

> N: I'm a colleague in her department and I want to do research with her. I want to have her full commitment and I'm not going to have that and, in fact, that's what's happened. It's been three years now. I think a part of me being upset about that was her not accepting my lifestyle as the lifestyle she would choose and I took that as a piece of rejection. And her interpretation which is hurtful is that I'm sorry that

I didn't have kids. So she sees my upsetness as me being jealous of her. And that's not my reading at all.

I: What's your reading?

N: That I'm disappointed in her (laughing). That, you know, she's done this. And I've lost a piece of her because I can't really know what that's (motherhood) all about. So it's a friendship issue . . . It takes a long time to find somebody who can be right there for you and she was real special, so I haven't felt that about other people having children. Like other women in my department aren't my kind of people so it makes more sense for them to have children (laughing).

Elaine, age 48

Elaine and Jo and Barb point to a larger loss than the loss of individual relationships; they all hint at losing social power and viability when friends rejected childlessness. Their example, their lives, are no longer considered important. Former friends' deep and appropriate concerns with the dailiness of motherhood shut them out. And, in a time of great emphasis on mothering, they seem to be anachronistic. They are not frontrunners, independent thinkers, or even alternative role models. Or, at least, that is their experience.

Wedges in friendships sometimes resulted when not–mothers felt their ideas about and contributions to children's lives discounted. As Isabel said to me, "you can only go so far when you are childless, as I'm sure you know too, without the message, 'you have no right to talk to me about this.'" Another woman reported her feeling that friends hesitated to leave their children at her house for the afternoon because they assumed she wouldn't know how to care for them. She talked of having had friends "with a baby in one arm and a book in the other, you know. That's how they learned." She felt she was competent to learn as well. Another participant complained:

If you express an opinion about school busing or if you express an opinion about public schools versus private schools, it's like, well, "what are you expressing your opinion for? You don't have any kids. You don't deserve an opinion on this." Instead of saying, "Well, maybe this person could be a little more objective because their own children aren't going to be affected." . . . They lose their social commitment and put all their commitment into their children . . . What they engage in is a lot of individual solutions to what I consider to be social problems. You know, they take their child out of the public school and put them in a private school so their child will get a better education. And don't look at how that affects the public schools in general. They just want to be sure that their child has a break in life. And they lose sight of the larger group of children. So a lot of times I think people that don't have children would make better school board members because they wouldn't feel like they had to do what was best for their individual child.

Maria, age 43

Obviously, not all not–parents are as socially concerned as Maria, and obviously not all parents are as socially unconcerned as she asserts. But her statement is a reminder that generalizing assumptions about parents and not–parents may be misleading. Both may have solidarity with children just as both may disregard child welfare.

Many of the narrators thus spoke with great emotion about the wedges that occurred in their intimate friendships with mothering women. Many also describe wedges with non-intimates, with women who were co-workers and casual acquaintances. Often these strains were directly tied to patriarchal policies and practices discriminating against mothers in the workplace:

I see at work a lot of women who have come back to work after having children. I see some of them that are sort of resentful of me, okay, because I am doing very well in my job and I have consistently gotten promotions and things like that. But I have the time for my job. They've come back to work, they're about my age, they're not where I am . . . It bothers me because if a man moved around like that or took time out, he would not have to start at the bottom. But unfortunately, that is the way the system works and I feel it's going to be a long time before it changes. But they do have a lot of resentment and feeling like I should be there too.

Rhonda, age 46

Wedges also showed up in voluntary associations. Lee Bishop spoke for several women who felt interested and comfortable talking about children whom they knew and cared about with the children's mothers, yet felt bored and excluded when children dominated the conversation at women's clubs or groups. "At some clubs that I used to join, women, you know, all they would do is talk about their children. I really try not to be near them because I'm bored."

Divisions showed up among feminists in political work groups. One woman, sympathetic to mothers, recounts the tensions she experiences:

> . . . In feminist meetings . . . the women with children feel that they are not accommodated or that those of us who don't have children don't understand the complications . . . It's very easy not to pay real close attention and then take action (disregarding) what they have to struggle and hassle with. We'll say, you know, we are having this meeting Sunday morning at 9 but we don't want any kids there. Like what are they suppose to do?
>
> Beth, age 44

Beth felt very connected in her relationships with mothers. Yet even in the most supportive relationships, occasional riffs may appear. For some women, permanent distances were reported; for others, breaks were minor or temporary. Claire offered a balanced perspective when speaking about the changes that occurred within her long-standing circle of friends when all became parents, except she and her partner. Claire reports seeing her friends less frequently and less spontaneously than before but she added:

> Has anything important happened between the relationship between the couples with them having kids and us not? No. Nothing important. A minor annoyance, nothing significant just, not annoyance, not irritation . . . We can just work around their schedules because we've got the freedom to do so. So it hasn't caused a problem.
>
> Claire, age 45

A humorous piece in *Parents* magazine is a reminder that con-flicts between mothers and not–mothers are not isolated events.[20] Drawing on stereotyped differences between Us (parents) and Them (not–parents), Deborah Heiligman writes, "*They* definitely do not understand *Us*":

> They exercise to fit into bikinis and miniskirts and skintight dresses. We exercise so that our hearts don't give out before college is paid for and to attempt to recover a trace of muscle tone before our next pregnancy.[21]

The women in my sample would conclude from this that parents don't understand not–parents either.

These tensions are related to the particular current form of social organization and its attendant ideology, one that encourages intense bonds between mothers and children and awesome, private responsibilities. Women who remain childless are, in some sense, advantaged, as they are not "held responsible" the way mothers are. Yet childless women may be treated as outsiders and experience symbolic censure and have their lives not treated seriously. Contemporary social practices and policies that create enclosed families disadvantage mothers and childless women differently while creating opposing privileges. And as Patricia Hill Collins reminds us, "privilege is often invisible to those who benefit from it."[22] Thus differing penalties and privileges accorded to contrasting reproductive preferences can divide women and keep us apart. Rather than supporting each other in our differing needs, we may separate as mothers and not–mothers. Rhonda recognized this reality when she said, "I find my freedom is a barrier with mothers."

A Complicated Freedom

Despite difficulties in social relations related to childlessness, the overwhelming majority of women in this study were clear on the key advantage of their not–mothering status. Narrators appreciated having "freedom from" the worries and responsibilities of raising children and they treasured having the "freedom to" develop creative and meaningful work lives, to find some measure of solitude, to have many choices:

> In contrast to other people, I think (childlessness has meant) a certain freedom—financial, time, ability to identify with career, ability to be good in what you're doing because you have the male–kind of time.
>
> Elaine, age 48

> Well, it's all in the area of freedom. I guess I look at our society now and our values and what's happening to kids. And I would just hate to have to deal with that on a day-to-day basis. Gee, I have to do the right thing with you so that you don't end up on drugs, you don't end up an alcoholic, you don't end up like that . . . That's a real big burden on somebody.
>
> Maria, age 43

> It was probably the best decision I've ever made for myself because it has affected everything else in a positive way . . . My decision has given me a great deal of personal freedom, to focus on my work and to be very creative in my work and not have any distractions. Well, I have distractions, but nothing of the magnitude that a child would be . . . I think (children) would have been a big barrier to my own growth and my creativity.
>
> Kay, age 46

> Well, it's mostly my freedom. It's meant that I have a lot of choices that I would not have. And that includes being lazy and sloppy and noisy. It's not that this has freed me to do the great things in life. Although certainly I could never do the things that I think are positive either. You know, people with kids can't stay up all night and sleep all day and they can't use four-letter words and they can't go to a bar and hang around. And I certainly think we would be financially strapped to have children and lead the kind of life we live.
>
> Jo, age 40

Women are referencing their freedom to the curtailment of mental and physical independence that the institution of motherhood often demands. Many of the participants in my sample remained childless, in part, as a strategy to gain at least some of "the freedom of male experience and possibility."[23] And this strategy *is* effective in that it can provide women with some measure of autonomy—financial and mental and physical. This is not to be underestimated in a culture where women are systematically subordinated and constrained. Each woman valued the real control she was able to exercise over her time and her life. The women speak of freedom from the worry and guilt that many mothers must increasingly bear, and of the freedom to make choices about their time, the ability to pursue avocations as well as various chosen personal and public involvements. Some narrators spoke about needing free space for the growth of their projects, a creative reverie not traditionally allowed women. And others spoke about the sheer pleasure of their time alone—in the garden, working in the kitchen, enjoying life at home alone. "Man, I'm in hog heaven," said Claire, describing her experience of being at home for an extended period by herself with no phones ringing. The fact that mothers, as a rule, experience less flexibility and self-determination, was not lost on this group. As one woman phrased it:

> This might be the only important thing I've said in three hours. I think it's a privilege that we need to acknowledge, that I need to acknowledge, maybe I just mean ease, because I have choices that mothers don't have. It's like taking for granted that you are white or taking for granted that you are educated or that you have a good living income and saying, "like well, it doesn't count." *It counts for everything*.
>
> Beth, age 44

For some participants, however, freedom was elusive as career demands stole every waking hour. Listen to Cathy, an intellectual who, frustrated by the low salaries in the educational field, took employment in the business sector:

> I'm in a sales job at [a major corporation]. I've been in the same position for seven years. It's not something that's so terrifically fulfilling right now, especially on an intellectual level. Keeps me probably too busy. It develops a part of me but I know there's a whole other part that's just lying fallow right now . . . It's not my life's purpose, but

it's probably something I spend fourteen hours a day on. I mean, I have too little time for anything else. So work in large businesses tends to pull you away from, perhaps the more fundamental things in life . . . I wish away the weeks because some of the work is so pressure-filled that I'm glad the week's over. It seems like a waste of time to spend so much time working and not enough time growing as a human being.

I realize now, as I have more and more material things that they wear you down. I have money from my job in a sense. We have security to a nominal degree. But it's the intellectual life that's the most rewarding and satisfying. And I don't mean just intellectual, being off in a tower. But you place such value in friendships, and a simple dinner together, and you know now we don't have time for that anymore.

Cathy, age 45

The following lament is from a woman who remained in an academic environment:

I've had these grants, I've really gotten focused on my career, and my problem is I've never been sicker in my life, sick all the time because I'm much too busy. I'm working just all the time. I have grants, a private practice, I do consulting, I'm on the faculty here, and God, last year I had two other jobs, it was just crazy . . . And I do a lot of traveling. I'm going to Vienna in three weeks, I'm going to Saratoga Springs next week, and I'm going to Reno next . . . You know I'm doing different things. I'm doing management now. Managing, doing my best, learning a lot of new things. I think I look at myself and I'm much where I want to be.

The downside is that I have to give up some things. I haven't had as good a time. I've always hated when people say, "How are you?" and you say, "Oh, busy, busy." I just get so tired of that in our culture. And I've become one of those people in the last couple of years because of the commitments.

Elizabeth, age 48

For these professionally-identified women, "the freedom of male experience and possibility" and "the male–kind of time" that Elaine spoke of above, can lead to not much freedom and no time, given the male–kind of institutions in which women must compete to succeed. For some women, the very freedom that they have achieved through limiting their domestic responsibilities has been lost in the public sphere. Remember too, many in this group of women described themselves as diligent, as deeply devoted to whatever work they took upon themselves. Ironically, women often ended up wanting more time for *themselves*. As Ellen phrased it: "I'd like more time for me that doesn't feel so frantically giving to everyone else."

In general, then, many in this group of women, by remaining childless, freed themselves from an oppressively-organized home only to be "free" to spend more of their time in an oppressively-organized marketplace. As Juliet Schor discusses in her book, *The Overworked American*,[24] in the past twenty years U.S. workers have seen their working hours increase by the equivalent of one month a year, leaving little time for leisure. Thus the "ability to identify with your career, ability to be good at what you're doing" was not always a clear benefit.

An additional time demand confronted these women. Although they escaped the particular injustices experienced by women who take on motherhood, they *are* daughters. They share with all women the burdens of an increasingly privatized system of care for the aging.[25]

For the first time in American history, the average married couple has more parents than children.[26] A report released in May of 1989 by the Older Women's League claims that American women spend an average of eighteen years helping parents and seventeen years caring for children.[27] Although there may be substantial differences in the amount of time involved in helping parents and caring for children, the point is that childless women as daughters may find themselves with expanding domestic responsibilities as they and their parents age.

For example, at the time of our interview, one woman's disabled mother had just moved in with her. "I'm taking care of my mother. Yes indeed. Breakfast, lunch and dinner. I spent two hours this morning getting a refrigerator upstairs and getting her prepared, meals prepared for today, and so forth and so on."

Women generally felt that because they were childless, "people assume that you have this gay, carefree life with no responsibilities attached." Some felt that the opposite was true:

> I think there is the assumption that if you don't have children you have all this *time* in your life. Because I know my sister will say to me, "What do you *do* all the time?" And I've often thought the opposite happens. That when you have children, the children are taking up hours so you tend to say, "no," or not even think about some things. But when you don't have children, I think about volunteer work and all the crazy things that I do.
>
> Donna, age 43

While women limited responsibilities in the private sphere, they often committed their time to activities in the public sphere. In short, although they used their time differently than mothers, they did not necessarily feel that they had more of it for themselves. Given the demands placed on women to provide care to family members and the demands of high-powered work and public commitments, the notion of freedom for some childless women remains, at best, a complicated one.

Conclusion

For most of the women I interviewed, childlessness was not part of daily conscious identity. As described earlier, women defined themselves by what they *did* do and *had done* rather than by what they had not achieved. Susan, who was interviewed for a book about pioneering women in the scientific field, said about that interview: "I never, never spoke about not having children. It never entered into it." But of course childlessness *did* enter into it; her life's work was critically dependent on her decision not to mother. This is a woman who devoted her life to her career, who occasionally lived apart from her husband. Given the period of history she lived through, her life would have been entirely different if she had had a child.

Susan's experience illustrates how remaining childless at one level means nothing to women as they identify themselves, since it is an absence not a presence. But at the same time, it counts for everything. When a woman does not exercise her reproductive potential, her social relations are transformed, shifts in gender power relations are created, and a unique set of pleasures and tensions, freedoms and constraints, results.

7

CONCLUSION

If we cannot imagine (or worse, no longer believe in) a culture where
the difference between mothers and nonmothers will be meaningless—because parenting will not require martyrdom and women's
humanity will not rise or fall depending on reproductive choices—
then we have succumbed to the pro-family onslaught. If we find it
impossible to state publicly that "the family" should have as many different forms and meanings as there are ways of envisioning
affectionate and sexual bonds among humans, then we have allowed
sexist anxieties to contaminate our vision of a truly human potential.

—Ellen Herman[1]

A WOMAN is a person. She may bear children; she may not. She
may rear children; she may not. She may be deeply concerned
about the lives of children or she may not, whether or not she is a
mother. Yet since the nineteenth century, motherhood has been
seen as the reason for women's existence. The collapse of womanhood into motherhood, I have argued, is inaccurate and morally
unacceptable. Maternalism splits the category "woman" into good
and bad, successful and failed, based on the primary reproductive
role. And maternalist ideology is employed to defend an unjust
patriarchal organization of private and social life which disempow-
ers mothers and not–mothers alike.

My special concern has been to describe the negative impact of
maternalist thinking on the lives of childless women. I have highlighted the context of *gender inequality* in which women become
mothers or remain not–mothers and the *reproductive politics* that
are generated by this inequality. My approach, then, has been to

view intentional childlessness as a social practice taking place in a highly politicized context, a practice which creates personal challenges for not–mothering women, and creates analytical challenges to existing theories about women.

In this concluding chapter, I summarize major personal challenges facing women without children and I review how discourses about motherhood and childlessness reinforce women's mothering. I end with reflections about securing a context in which reproductive diversity is sustained.

The Personal Challenges Facing Not–mothering Women

The personal challenges of childlessness are deeply rooted in not–mothering women's contradictory relationship to patriarchal ideology and social organization. The women I interviewed confronted subtle yet pervasive prejudices and social institutions antagonistic to their needs. Individual women worked to negotiate these pressures.

The identity offered to childless women, despite historical fluctuations, remains a deficient one. This symbolic degradation creates risks to comfort and security; yet the disadvantage also creates opportunities for the development of a solid sense of self that is not dependent on cultural approval. Most not–mothers I spoke with saw themselves as competent and complete women, with a network of gratifying relationships. For some, cultural messages aimed at childless women held no power—they were easily rejected. For others, sensitivity to popular meanings of childlessness required negotiation. In both cases the task of coming to terms with nonconformity required internal, interpersonal, and social self-assertion—and affirmation—in the face of opposition.

One good example of the necessity for self-assertion is revealed as not–mothers are called upon, in a regular fashion, to account for their noncompliance with a central mandate of marriage. Although sensitivity to other people's inquiries varied, not–mothers found it impossible to avoid engaging in "explanatory work." Women developed various strategies to deal with the ubiquitous "children question" in order to reduce its most stressful aspects. Creating satisfactory personal explanations for childlessness was for some women difficult, thus making explanatory work a continuing internal struggle and external hassle. For others it wasn't important or especially difficult. In either case, no woman could escape engaging in this work that often took place in an unsympathetic atmosphere.

As women mediated the gap between their own felt experiences and others' stereotypical representations of childless women, they commonly reversed standard meanings assigned to mothers and not–mothers. Indeed, one of the most striking characteristics of my conversations with narrators was the sheer volume of reverse discourse. For example, reacting to the charge of selfishness, participants were quick to resist the judgment and point out their pro-social behaviors. And it was not uncommon for them to link their sense of fulfillment to their childless status, contradicting the view that not–mothers live empty lives and that motherhood is required to make a life full. This reverse discourse provided a positive sense of self for childless women, although it did not set conditions for positive relations with mothers.

Women often, with considerable passion, described the "wedges" that occurred in their friendships with mothers. Not–mothers looked on their female friends as primary relationships, as key sources of emotional connection. When their friends became mothers, they sometimes felt themselves placed in a secondary position in their friends' lives, causing hard feelings and a sense of loss. Further, the gender division of labor creates a women's subculture characterized by strong bonds based in the common work of childbearing and rearing.[2] Narrators felt left behind when friends became mothers, and felt left out when in a group of mothers. These tensions among women, generated by reproductive difference, have not been the focus of much research. Gerson argues that "politically consequential social divisions are emerging among women based not on traditional class or ethnic cleavages but rather on differences in women's work and family circumstances."[3] Further attention could provide additional evidence concerning the ways that promulgation of a single gender norm may paradoxically divide women from each other.

Additionally, childless women who wanted children in their lives found it difficult to establish and maintain permanent intergenerational ties. A significant proportion did have important relationships with children, but extending these to long-term connections that could withstand geographical separations was hard because of the absence of kinship assumptions.

It is not surprising that the majority of not–mothers I spoke with were challenged by moments or periods of internal questioning related to their childlessness. Women experienced times when their emotional comfort was interrupted by "rumblings," second thoughts about not having children. These rumblings were not considered problematic in some ongoing way, but rather as temporary musings or wistful feelings that happened from time to time depending on circumstances. Mothers also have their moments of doubt about their road taken, depending on circumstances, but mothers' rumblings are a very small part of the public discourse about mothering. The implicit suggestion is that not–mothers think (regretfully) about not having children but mothers don't consider possible losses incurred by their choices. Thus motherhood is reinforced.

The organization of dependent care within a privatized family setting generated stress for some participants. Mutual assistance and obligation are assumed and enforced between parents and children. Social policies and programs expect and encourage this contribution of adult children's care to aging parents. This apparently leaves the childless elderly to fend for themselves. The unspoken message is, "Okay, you want independence, you've *got* independence." Although the risk of isolation is greater for the childless, it does not necessarily follow that individual childless women will become more isolated than their mothering counterparts.[4] Childless women, *because* they cannot fall back on children, are planners. Individual women trembled at the thought of ending up in a public institution for the aged. Having money and social networks was seen as a protection against the worst-case fears. And even though most of the participants could identify a person or persons outside the marital relationship they could count on for assistance—their real and potential future supports—these supports (especially non-kin ties) are not socially recognized. The oldest women interviewed spoke for many saying that having children would make later life *easier.* Yet all were quick to reaffirm their childlessness and thought having children as social insurance was a selfish act. They coped with their worries by careful planning.

A practical dilemma childless women faced was inventing alternatives to standard rules of inheritance. Women's estate planning, although not the same emotional issue as future care, was problematic. Some of the women had put off writing a will since they simply weren't sure what to do. Others developed ways of distributing their resources that crossed class lines and included non-kin individually and/or collectively through contributions to friends and various social organizations.

The advantage of remaining childless that participants most often identified—"freedom"—was indeed a clear benefit for them but, in some cases, posed an ironic challenge. Not–mothers appreciated the real and emotional time available to them. Personal growth, relationship with spouse, creative work, political activism, and social life all benefitted from flexibility and spontaneity. By limiting their responsibilities in the domestic sphere these women escaped some of the oppressive aspects of the institution of motherhood. However, this freedom provided more time for activity in the competitive and often alienating public sphere. Thus some women with highly satisfying and committed public lives still found themselves overcommitted and overworked. Such a work life, often combined with increasing responsibilities for aging parents and relatives, left some women still seeking that illusive goal—"freedom."

To summarize, women who remain childless must forge and live out an alternative path. Their lives contradict central assumptions about women's nature and appropriate social location. This impacts on identity and development, family, social and interpersonal relations, and the life course. The women I interviewed were up to the challenges.

Taken together, stories collected from intentional not–mothers go beyond providing insights into their own experiences; they call into question theories that construct the desire to mother as primarily psychologically reproduced and stable. Their narratives reveal social forces that relate to the subversion of such reproduction, and they reveal the way women's interests and energies are regulated in a routine fashion in the direction of childbearing and childrearing. Such knowledge must be incorporated into feminist frameworks and strategies aimed at understanding and changing the existing power relations between women and men in society.

Discourses on Motherhood/Childlessness and the Social Production of Mothering

The experiences described by intentionally childless women not only contradict the notion that the "reproduction of mothering" is inevitable; they reveal the "insidious and often paradoxical pathways of modern social control"[5] that are obscured by theorizing which relies on psychoanalytic insights alone. Women are not only *pulled* (attracted) to mothering; women are *pushed* (forced) in this direction, in part by cultural representations of both motherhood and childlessness (even though not all women are equally pulled and/or pushed). A "normal" life for a married woman includes motherhood; not having children is, for most, "an unthinkable option."[6]

Poststructuralists understand that desire is produced through "discourses" which exist in written, oral, and visual forms and in the social practices of everyday life. Consciousness, language, and meaning figure centrally into the construction of identity as do social institutions. In this view, there is no reason to privilege early psychosexual relations above other forms of social relations when considering the pull towards mothering.[7] Poststructural assumptions open up an approach which is historically and socially specific and which assumes female desire is open to change.[8]

Over the past decade, Chodorow's theory of the reproduction of mothering, along with the works of other mothering theorists, has extended significantly the normalization of female mothering.

Through the construction of the desire for motherhood as universal and fixed early in life, these discourses, ironically, may participate in the very processes of male domination they seek to expose. The cultural conception of woman as mother is reinforced as the norm, and motherhood becomes the standard against which all women are measured. In short, all women are assigned a single identity.

My central theoretical claim is that the desire to mother does not exist outside of or prior to language and cultural images of motherhood, but is brought into play by how we talk and think and represent both motherhood and childlessness. In this view, the dominant feminist theories on mothering may be understood as historically specific discourses which privilege mothering women as normal, thus placing constraints on reproductive autonomy. A key poststructural premise is that meaning is created through implicit or explicit contrast. Just as the term "woman" depends on its counterpart "man" for its definition, "childless woman" acquires its cultural significance in relation to the meanings assigned to motherhood. Childless woman is not–mother, just as "woman is not–man; as such, she is 'other' to that which is the norm."[9]

The risk in contemporary feminist perspectives is that they may be employed to present mothering as women's ultimate fulfillment and highest priority.[10] These beliefs are legitimated through discourses which represent childlessness as an inferior status. These opposing *meanings* assigned to motherhood and to childlessness, and the institutional and social practices that maintain such meanings, figure prominently into the reproduction of mothering. Individual women are biased towards motherhood in order to experience symbolic (and real) benefits and to avoid the symbolic (and real) penalties involved in remaining childless. Women who remain childless must push against symbolic and materially-based pro-mothering practices. In daily life, as we have learned, childlessness is associated with certain benefits, just as motherhood has costs. But these experiences are lost in the symbolic world of maternalist politics. Women, and reproductive choice, are the losers.

These discourses, then, which construct childless women as inferior nurturers and as unfinished women, have a policing function.

They play a role in women's decisions *to* have children and they do create anxiety for some not–mothers. The assignment of negative traits and emotions to not–mothers regulates desire. Women are directed to accept an institution of motherhood which enables male dominance and refuses autonomy to women. Nonconformist women are "disciplined" by these beliefs. Those women who described episodes of emotional discomfort most often described struggles with dominant cultural representations, not with missing relationships. Women also described materially-based concerns, of potential or real isolation in later life, based on social practices that privilege and assume kin ties over other social relations.

The poststructural project is not to reverse the opposition by calling for the superiority of childlessness, but, in the words of Mary Poovey, to "problematize the very idea of opposition"[11] and the notion of some stable and fixed meaning. The accounts of childless women help us do this. These stories, as I understand them, challenge the fixed view that childless women are all incomplete and unloving while mothers are all fulfilled and caring. This is not to imply that reproductive differences are meaningless. Mothers and not–mothers occupy different social locations and experience a different set of pleasures and dilemmas, just as they share common problems.

Since motherhood and childlessness exist in hierarchical opposition to each other, whatever "childlessness" means at any particular historical moment depends on the meanings of "motherhood." What is needed now are new ways to envision and practice reproductive distinctions. In simple terms, we need to sever a false polarity between mothers and not–mothers while not ignoring differing needs. And we need a social community and public policies that support these aims.

Toward Reproductive Diversity

At present, maternalist ideology holds individual women within private households responsible for the care and nurture of dependent others, supposedly making collective responsibility unnecessary and inappropriate. Women, defined by their motherly qualities, are accountable for the day-to-day care of children, aging parents, sick and disabled family members, with little support from the larger community. Naturally loving women make a loving community superfluous. These exertions of love, glorified in speech, but economically unsupported, reproduce a class system for mothers and children.

Mothers obviously lose. It is hard to pursue goals independent of caretaking work. Children lose too, a fact reflected in the astonishingly high rate of child poverty in the United States. And as this book documents, women who do not assume their place as mothers, while materially advantaged, are maligned in other ways. Unwomanly conduct is morally scrutinized, while the immoralities of current gender and childrearing arrangements are accepted and reinforced. Maternalism is a thought pattern that also insults men and limits their human growth by discouraging them from developing nurturant potentials.

As an alternative to the status quo, we must continue the ancient struggle for the creation of a just society. We must establish a humanity–enhancing culture where we *expect* caring relationships to extend beyond women and beyond the walls of individual households. In the future, there will be more "couple nests," more women single parenting, more late life citizens living alone. And there will continue to be people who are not in partnerships. Our households are small units, containers too meager to meet all the human needs of their members. Women who are mothers need societal supports, and the support of other adults around them, especially when their children are young; women without children need supportive community as they age. All women (and children and men) need meaningful bonds with others and the opportunity to pursue idiosyncratic goals independent of those bonds. For individuals to experience both intimacy and autonomy, the work of nurturing and maintaining human beings must be collectively shared.

Barbara Katz Rothman warns that without collective responsibility, and with the growth of technology, children become products, commodities, and parents become private owners.[12] She contends that in order to protect children's interests, nurturance must be coupled to social relations rather than biological ties:

> We can focus on nurturant, caring, human relations. We can come to accept and to respect a wider variety of family relationships and arrangements. Those qualities we have come to think of as maternal could become more widely shared, by both men and women. We could direct this nurturance, this maternal caring, not just to children, but to each other.[13]

Nurturance would then become the province of all people, not just mothers. This respects and appreciates the support that not–mothers (and men, older children, and older adults) provide, and takes the pressure off women who are raising children as a central activity. These social relations require social support through wide-ranging public policies that take us in the direction of wage justice, more cooperative housing, widely available health care, and monetary and social supports for dependent young, old, and disabled citizens. Under such conditions, choices about children will be less a matter of sacrifice for individual women, regardless of which choice they make. These needed changes provide for diversity and at the same time present a set of goals around which women can come together and organize *because of*—rather than in spite of—such diversity.

Feminists suggest ways of opening up a variety of nurturing options and of better recognizing existing nonparental caring relationships. The writings of some African–American feminists discourage the division of women into separate and exclusive reproductive categories. Patricia Hill Collins posits child nurturing continuums and recognizes the contributions of childless women to the lives of mothers and children as she recognizes the not–mothering work of mothers. Blood mothers are not the only women who raise or bond with children; other–mothers and community other–mothers (who may or may not be blood mothers) are visible in her discussions of parenting. bell hooks talks about being a "pretend mother" to her "play daughter," and she mentors many younger women who are not kin. Asserting that individualism threatens the well-being of African–Americans and that black people need "an ethic of communalism to live with dignity and integrity," hooks speaks to other black women: "Concurrently, in our roles as mothers, or as 'pretend' mothers (people like me who do not have blood children but who joyously adopt and parent here and there), we can do so much to transform the violence and pain in black life by giving peace and understanding, by showing compassion."[14] Here hooks' concepts smudge the barriers between women who are mothers and women who are not. And her words are for all women.

Feminists who call for co-parenting with men extend the term "mother" to men. For Sara Ruddick, men who do mothering work become mothers. And Diane Ehrensaft describes how her children refer to both she and her male partner as "mommy." This also extends nurturing to men, quite appropriately.

There is a difficulty here, however. With the word mother potentially extended to childless women and men (and to child care workers, teachers, older siblings, and older adults), at some point nearly everyone becomes a mother. This, perhaps, is a good problem from the perspective that I am arguing. But do we want to continue to connect caring with the female gender role? Ann Snitow captures the dilemma when she asks: "Do we want this presently capacious identity, mother, to expand or to contract? How special do we want mothering to be? In other words, what does feminism gain by the privileging of motherhood?"[15]

The values associated with motherhood—protection, compassion, supportive warmth, and reliable care[16]—are not the problem. Who can oppose the realization of such values? I, for one, want to live in a world where such values are operationalized, not only adored. We need to affirm the virtues that are associated with motherhood as we sever them from their longtime confinement to the feminine gender role. Expected to inhabit the entire human community, women will be both responsible to others through intimate bonds and active citizenship, and they will be freer to pursue goals unrelated to directly nurturing others.

In the struggle for reproductive diversity, this affirmation of the values of human warmth must be combined with collective recognition and encouragement of women's nonbiological competencies and achievements.[17] As M. Elizabeth Tidball wrote in 1979, given scientific advances, women who in the past were expected to make motherhood the centers of their lives, now have "additional or alternative purposes in the world."[18] For some women, motherhood may be "a nonessential ingredient in their lives."[19] Indeed, my research documents the existence of such women. Yet the social order has not regularly valued women's nonbiological creations and has not welcomed the idea of women having "alternative purposes in the world."

Our just society will affirm and promote the development of women's autonomous talents. It will allow women routes to productivity and creativity other than through parenting. It will welcome new identities as "selves-in-community." And it will foster the understanding that we are *all* blood relations.

A just society is not merely a utopian dream. In this period of great social change we must work towards a more expansive sense of humanity and resist a return to narrow understandings of women's possibilities. In the twenty-first century society we help to create, relatedness and liberation will be compatible. Only then will reproductive freedom mean more than when and how.

APPENDIX:
ABOUT THE RESEARCH

To pursue promising ways of understanding our experience is not necessarily to seek "Truth" or power in an Enlightenment sense. Rather it entails a commitment to responsibility and a hope that there are others "out there" with whom conversation is possible.

—Jane Flax[1]

R ESEARCHERS are often criticized for using methods which are not clearly stated and explained.[2] What follows here is a full description of my research process, including problems encountered and decisions made to deal with them. My hope is that this detailed discussion of procedures will help qualitative scholars as we collectively refine strategies and deepen insights.

The Sample

I originally set out to locate forty married, intentionally childless women. I wanted to recruit two distinct age cohorts. The midlife group would be comprised of twenty women between the ages of 45 and 55, the later life group comprised of twenty women between the ages of 65 and 75. Such a design would allow study of not–mothering women at two different points along the life course and in two different locations in history.

I knew that finding a sample of married, not–mothering women would be a challenging task: the population is small and has low visibility and the subject matter of the research is sensitive. The time and cost of probability sampling of such a population was prohibitive. Thus, I decided to identify respondents through a strategy which combined two distinct qualitative sampling techniques: network sampling and advertising. In the network sampling procedure used and described by both Lillian Rubin[3] and Pamela Daniels and Kathy Weingarten,[4] a number of women who live within a limited geographical area and whose characteristics fit those required by the research are interviewed and then asked for the names of other like women. Those individuals on the list with the most distant geographical and emotional connections to the respondent are then contacted for participation in the project. This technique guards against the bias of a sample composed of friendship groups and is economically feasible.

In practice, this procedure did not work well for me. I started interviewing women I personally knew to be married and intentionally childless. Not one woman I interviewed could give me a *list* of names of like women. If I was lucky, she would suggest a name of someone who "might" fit all the requirements. Usually the name given was not a close friend but an acquaintance: someone who worked at the same university, a well-known local figure such as a lawyer or doctor, or a woman known through common membership in a community association or group. Age and whether childlessness was voluntary or involuntary were rarely known. It soon became clear that I need not worry about a sample composed of friendship groups.

I did follow up on whatever names were given to me by those I interviewed. Thus "snowball sampling"[5] became one method I used to locate participants. In all cases I sent a letter introducing myself, my project, and requirements for participation. I enclosed a form, with a stamped self-addressed envelope, that allowed women to choose participation or no participation. I made follow-up phone calls to those who were willing to be interviewed.

The age constraints I placed on participation became a problem immediately. For instance, through a referral I located one woman who turned out to be fifty-nine years old. She didn't fit the age requirement as she was between the mid and later life age groups. Finding women to interview was proving difficult, especially women past the age of fifty. I could not let the opportunity pass. I abandoned the idea of two groups and interviewed anyone over forty who was willing to participate. I lowered the age requirement since I had located several women who were in their early forties and wanted to become part of the project. I made sure that women in their early forties were firmly committed to their childless status.

I expected that locating later life women would pose real difficulties. Virtually no studies of this specific population exist to suggest data sources. I decided to reach out to local community groups that served a later life population. I spoke with six different American Association of Retired Persons chapters in the Greater Buffalo area and had announcements placed in chapter newsletters; I talked to senior citizen center directors, managers of various retirement homes, gerontological social workers. I placed an announcement in the Western New York Network In Aging; I advertised in *Common Ground,* Western New York Women's Newsjournal. Results were disappointing. Research announcements did not provide needed participants. Most professionals and administrators I spoke with were interested and tried to be helpful but none could turn up names of older women I might contact.[6] I decided to recruit and interview in two other geographic locations: the Philadelphia area and the Northern New Jersey/New York City area. Since I had graduate school and family in Philadelphia and family in New York and New Jersey, these were areas I visited on a regular basis. I would coordinate interviewing with family visiting.

I decided to advertise in national newsletters. I sent research announcements to the Association for Women in Psychology newsletter and the Association for Women in Social Work newsletter. I did this in part because I was a member of these groups and announcements could be placed free of charge. I placed paid ads in *The NASW News,* in *Broomstick* (a journal by and for women over 40), and in *Hot Flash* (a health newsletter for older women). I also placed an announcement in the S.O.W.N. Newsletter (The Supportive Older Women's Network, Inc., in Philadelphia).

Although I specified Western New York, Philadelphia, and the New York City area, I received responses from women from all over the country who were interested in being interviewed. This proved useful at a later date when I decided to do telephone interviewing as well as face-to-face interviews.

Through responses from research announcements and suggestions from family members, close to one third of my final sample originated from the New York/New Jersey/Philadelphia area. During 1987 and into 1988, summer vacations and winter holiday visits with family were punctuated with scheduled interviews. In addition, my cousin in Rhode Island placed a research announcement in a women's networking newsletter and turned up two women willing to be interviewed. I thus vacationed in Rhode Island during the summer of 1988. Even my niece's wedding in the Boston area that fall provided me with the opportunity to do an interview. I traveled no place for a year without my tape recorder and research agenda.

Since it was decidedly costly and time-consuming to do face-to-face interviews all over the Northeast, and since I received responses from women in California, Michigan, and New Mexico, I decided to do telephone interviewing. My conversations followed the same format as the in-person interviews, lasted approximately two hours, and were taped. In the end, I conducted eight phone interviews and twenty-six in-person interviews. As mentioned earlier, my final sample included thirty-four women: three in their seventies, one in her sixties, two in their fifties, nineteen between the ages of forty-five and forty-nine, and the remaining nine were in their early forties. All were European–American except for one Latina.

The Interview

The recovery and interpretation of women's lives is an ongoing concern of feminist scholarship. Listening to women's stories and learning from their experiences has been critical to feminist recon-structions of knowledge.[7] I decided I would conduct in-depth interviews lasting approximately two hours. I would use an inter-view schedule but would not tightly structure the conversation. I would ask open-ended questions that allowed for thoughtful and elaborate responses.

As previously mentioned, I decided to ask each participant to complete a brief written autobiographical exercise before the inter-view. My own experience as a journal writer and facilitator of journal writing workshops made me aware of the advantages of written exercises as aids to organizing and understanding one's own experiences. An adaptation of an Intensive Journal exercise was used which instructed women to think about their lives as a book and to name eight or ten periods or "chapters."[8]

Although I had some initial reservations about making this extra demand on women's time, this step in the research process proved useful. Commonly, women voiced their interest and pleasure in doing the exercise; I liked the organization it imposed on the inter-view. I was also glad that women came to the interview with something to report. Rather than my starting out the interview asking questions and the interviewee responding, in most cases the interview started with the narrator having equal charge of the process, reading her chapters and then discussing each one. This established a comfortable and equitable interviewing situation from the start.

Several issue categories provided themes around which conversa-tions were organized. The experience of childlessness had a central place within the interview. How, when, and why the decision was made, emotions surrounding the decision, pressures to mother and not to mother, changes in how it feels to be childless with advanc-ing years, gratifications and/or regrets, "coming to terms" experiences, the inheritance question, and other matters were explored. Perceived changes associated with aging and one's sense of identity were also discussed.

When interviews took place in the Buffalo area I asked women if they preferred to meet at my home or at their home or workplace.

Four women chose to come to my residence, four invited me to their homes, four were interviewed where they worked. As I branched out to other geographical areas, women were most often interviewed in their own homes.

Women were remarkably gracious. A number of women asked me to be their guests for a meal. Questioning the wisdom of interviewing and eating at the same time, I accepted several invitations to share lunch after the interview was completed. In one case, my partner and I were the invited dinner guests of a participant and her partner in their retirement home dining room.

In the first two interviews, I was committed to the idea of a conversational style. Since women knew that I was intentionally childless, I was self-disclosing and interactive. I did not distance myself as an interviewer, and went out of my way to create an equal power relationship. I had theoretical grounding for this approach from some feminist writings. Ann Oakley's article, "Interviewing Women: A Contradiction in Terms?"[9] is an example of feminist writing which validates a conversational style and equitable sharing during the interview process.

As I read those first transcribed interviews, however, I noticed that it didn't help the data collection procedure to have so much of myself in the interview. I backed off. I always answered women's direct questions but did not offer my comments, ideas, or experiences when not solicited. I noticed that once women were into telling their own stories, they seemed perfectly happy to have someone listen and not interrupt. Thus, the interviews became very focused on the participant's experiences, as now seems only sensible, and I learned to bite my tongue when the impulse to share surfaced.

For a social worker conducting in-depth interviews, drawing the line between research and therapy can be challenging. I had to curb my urges to make "therapeutic interventions" as women presented their stories. For the most part, I was successful. In one case, however, when a woman at the end of our interview presented what seemed to me an unnecessarily negative summary of her life, I offered an alternative interpretation. I later received an appreciative note from her. I interviewed only one woman who was in immediate pain about her childless status. In this case, I shared some similar feelings. At the end of the interview she thanked me and said, "This conversation is the best thing that's happened to me in months!"

Adventures in Reading

At the same time that I started collecting data I spent long hours reading the latest in feminist scholarship. Although I had written a brief dissertation proposal in which I identified my research approach as a feminist one, I lacked a particular shaping framework. I needed models of research that could provide both inspiration and direction.

I started with feminist journals. I reviewed recent issues of *Signs* and *Feminist Studies* and read articles that dealt directly with theory. It became immediately clear that feminists were utilizing recent poststructural developments in the theory of language, subjectivity, and power to analyze various workings of patriarchy. I wanted to know more about the intersection between feminism and poststructuralism. I collected numerous books and articles on the subject.

Initially, much of what I read was barely understandable. Over time, however, I became familiar with the language and concepts. The poststructural emphasis on diversity and on theorizing difference fit perfectly with my scholarly intentions. I went back and forth between my data and my books. I counted on the readings I was doing to provide models of good scholarship as well as ideas that could direct my thinking.

Certain books or articles became what I call "sacred texts."[10] I returned to them again and again as I worked my data. I also kept buying and reading new books and journals. I kept notes on my readings and I kept notes on how these readings connected to my project. These memos were kept in my dissertation journal, which I describe in some detail later in this appendix.

About two-thirds of the way through the research process the reading became more problematic than beneficial. I was excited by the work being produced by feminists but they were producing too much! There was always a new book on the horizon that related to my theoretical interests. At some point it became clear that I had to do less reading. It was time to focus on what I had learned—and learn to ignore what I did not yet know. I had to concentrate on my own analysis and writing.

Data Organization and Analysis

At the start of my research, I intended to follow a qualitative method devised by sociologist Lillian Rubin and reported in her book, *Women of a Certain Age: The Midlife Search for Self.*[11] In her procedure interviews are tape recorded. Immediately following the interview, the tapes are reviewed and relevant parts transcribed verbatim. The notes and transcripts are then cut up, organized, and filed according to an initial list of categories. The list of categories is expanded as this process proceeds.

Rubin argues that this way of handling the data forces the researcher to think about the material while it is still fresh, and provides the opportunity for including whatever ideas she or he may have about it. Two files are kept on each category: descriptive and analytic. Thus much of the final analysis is a product of the "continuing process of recording, refining, and reformulating as the data of the interviews are organized and prepared for transcription."[12] Aspects of this process did not work for me for several reasons. First, I did not have the required reserves of time and energy after the interview to follow Rubin's procedure. I was surprised at how draining the interviews were. After two hours of intense concentration focused on emotionally charged material with an unknown person, I commonly felt exhausted. I needed a period of recovery before I could engage the review. To attend to and transcribe portions of a two-hour taped interview, take notes, and expand categories and files, both analytical and descriptive, took me eight to ten or more hours. Some days I conducted two interviews, which would take the whole day. In addition, analytical activity demanded what I call "quality think–time." For me, such time occurs in the morning when I am most alert, rested, and able to concentrate deeply for many hours at a stretch.

I did develop a minimal post-interview analysis method using a basic journal writer's device, "flow writing." This technique can be described as: "Write fast, write everything, include everything, write from your feelings, write from your body, accept whatever comes."[13] This allows spontaneous, honest writing; uncensored thoughts and feelings are "caught." In a sense, it is the opposite of careful, systematic thinking. This initial written exercise was useful in making conscious my own assumptions and became an important part of the raw material that later was scrutinized analytically. I usually spent no more than fifteen to twenty minutes jotting down as quickly as possible my impressions of the interview: feelings, key words that came to me, ideas to pursue, judgments I had, particular parts of the conversation or nonverbal behaviors that stood out and so on. The point is not to ponder or to think analytically, but to write from one's feelings.

Early on I also decided to veer from Rubin's approach of partial transcription because I did not yet have a sense of what was relevant and what was not. I had only the broadest and most descriptive categories, such as "self-descriptions," "stresses," and "aging issues." In short, I had no criteria yet developed to decide relevancy. Thus I decided to transcribe each interview in its entirety. This was time-consuming when I did the transcribing and costly when I had the help of others. But this was, as it turned out, a key decision. Having full transcripts available expanded my research opportunities; not only was the substance of women's accounts available for analysis, the accounts themselves became data to be analyzed. It was in the long hours pouring over the interviews, sentence by sentence, that the contests over meaning and the political importance of the discourse became starkly evident. I read women's accounts "not as reflections of truth or lie with respect to a pre-given real, but as instruments for the exercise of power, as paradigmatic enactments of struggles over . . . meaning."[14]

Initially, the "cut up and file" procedure Rubin describes also posed problems for me. I wanted to leave the interviews whole, intact. As I fragmented each interview into various categories I felt I was losing the contextual richness I was seeking. I decided to make two copies of each original transcript. One I kept in a file with the woman's first name and last initial. I also kept the flow writing exercise I did after each interview in this file, along with the woman's written exercise and the "Agreement to Participate" form. The other copy was available for cutting up.

In the early days of transcript reading, when I did not yet know exactly how to proceed, my impulse was to get the best understanding of each woman and her story that I could. I read through each transcript several times and produced a written summary. I wanted to take her on her own terms, stand in her own shoes as it were, before analyzing and picking away at her life. My recorded impressions after the interview obviously reflected my own assumptions and judgments. I wondered how insightful or arbitrary these impressions were. How much was "me" and how much was "her"? In short, just how accurate were my impressions?

I felt at times the fact that I was intentionally childless with my own story to tell might negatively influence my readings of the women I was interviewing. For example, my own story involves much more ambivalence than I generally encountered among participants. After about my seventh interview with women who evinced little self-doubt about their choice, I wrote in my journal, "Well, I've decided that *all* these women *can't* be lying!"

Since I was the "research instrument" I decided to attend to my own assumptions. I decided to do a written "dialogue" with each woman I interviewed.[15] The dialogue is a conversation (created by yourself) to help you gain insight into a person you wish to understand better. In the dialogue you simply address the subject and allow her to speak back to you in response. I discovered that this personal journal technique, when used as a research tool, allows the researcher to discover her assumptions and biases about the person interviewed as well as unacknowledged assumptions about her own frame of reference.

These dialogues were invaluable tools in increasing my sensitivity and skill as a researcher. They assisted me in uncovering and challenging my own unacknowledged assumptions and also in learning to respect the integrity of the women I interviewed. Participants "spoke back" to me, most of the time with harsh words, forcing me to question my instant analyses. My words, spoken in their voices, sent me back to the transcripts to check out the plausibility of my assumptions. I did not dialogue with every participant. I used the technique when I had either strong or confused reactions to the interview.

My journal was a key part of the research process. I kept an 8 1/2" by 11" unlined, bound artist's sketchbook as my "dissertation journal." It was in this book that I did my dialogues. I also captured spontaneous ideas and insights that came to me at unexpected times no matter how far afield they seemed. (The daily shower became the place where I had some of my best insights, after I had labored on the dissertation half a day.) I also took notes in this journal on the theoretical readings I was doing concurrently with the interviews.

By the time a third of the interviews were done, two problems emerged. One was the amount of data I was generating that needed to be contained and organized. With an approximately sixty-page transcript for each interview, and my own written summaries and notes on each woman, my files were thickening. And I already had over one hundred pages of journal musings. A second problem was treating each interview holistically and each interviewee respectfully. Now it was time to decide what was important, what was not important. And it was time to coordinate data across interviews.

To deal with these two issues, I returned to Rubin's filing system, with modifications. In addition to a master file on each woman, I developed category files slowly, and cross-referenced information from the interviews. I started out cutting the extra copy of the transcript I had made; this proved time-consuming and awkward. It was just as easy to jot a note, such as "Doris, p. 34. Busy—others see as compensation," and place the note in the file labeled, "Compensatory Ideology."

I then decided to cut up the dissertation journal and file each page in the appropriate category file. I discarded redundant—or what I deemed unimportant—notes. I developed preliminary chapter files, such as "methods chapter," "conceptual chapter," "introduction," and "conclusion." I then placed notes on readings I had done and my written ideas into these chapter files.

I initially tried keeping two files on each category, one descriptive and one analytic. But this did not work well since for me description and analysis often seemed to go together. For example, when I did cut up a transcript, I circled descriptive statements and made analytic statements in the margins. To separate the description from the analysis of that description made no sense to me. I ended with 34 master files (names of women) and 33 category files. When I went to work on each chapter, I pulled the category files that seemed most fitting and read through them. Some of these category files became fat, others had one or two slips of paper at most. In this way, relevant categories emerged while others receded quite visibly.

Although I had an outline as a guide, I wrote each chapter more or less as a free-standing "article." With no experience writing such a long document, I did what I knew how to do. In the end this posed problems. I had created a certain amount of redundancy since what I wrote in a previous chapter I often judged better placed in a later chapter. In the end, I had all the pieces of the puzzle but they had to be fit together.

As chapters were completed, they were put in a file with the chapter name. These completed chapter files were the place I kept ongoing ideas and citations to be incorporated into the final draft. Considerable revision was necessary as the end process of research. I sharpened the analysis; I deleted repetitions; I built links between chapters; I coordinated and rewrote parts of the introduction and the conclusion.

In summary, data collection, organization, and analysis proceeded simultaneously. Difficulties were resolved as they arose. The research process involved a dynamic interplay of scholarly reading, interviewing, deep reflection and journal writing, and organization and analysis of data.

Validity and Interpretation

It is both an exciting time and a confusing time to be doing qualitative research that must make knowledge claims. In the past several decades, arguments across the disciplines against empirical science have led to its currently deteriorated condition.[16] The latest approaches in feminist criticism, influenced by poststructural thinking, imply the abandonment of the concept of objective knowledge. Yet if objectivity is abandoned, how can one justify one's claims to knowledge? Lacking criteria of truth and falsehood, how can one judge the adequacy of our methods and theories?[17]

It is the researcher's capacity to "invite, compel, stimulate or delight the audience"[18] that makes a method useful. The point is to render problematic taken-for-granted ways of understanding the world and self-evident truths. Thus, the analyst's task includes offering radically different definitions of the world which startle and shock the reader and which focus awareness on the taken-for-granted nature of what is considered normative.

If the above criteria are accepted, my success as a researcher rests not with my ability to present to the reader the "truth" but rather "a best understanding,"[19] and a convincing argument that opens up thoughtful conversation about the role of reproductive difference in the maintenance of sexual inequality.

From Thesis to Book

A doctoral dissertation is not a book for publication. This study published by Routledge is a new work, based on but not the same as my thesis.

Writing the book involved various activities. Anonymous reviews helped guide my plans for revision. I decided to delete some chapters and expand others. Since two years had lapsed between finishing the thesis and starting the book, I returned to the feminist scholarship, finding new writings and new insights. I also did thorough bibliographic searches for recent data on childlessness. I returned to the interviews, rereading and elaborating on previous analysis. I wrote articles and received comments which assisted in the process. I decided to include more direct quotations from women. As I rewrote and reworked material, a new organizational structure emerged. By the end of my revisions, most of the original manuscript had been rewritten.

While I was working on revision, I sent a nine page research summary report to the narrators, inviting their response. I explained that the research project would be published, and in order to protect their confidentiality I asked them each to choose an altered identity. I gave women the option of falsifying their geographical location and their vocation as well. I also invited women to attend a gathering at my home to meet each other and further discuss my "results."

The response was excellent. Twenty-eight out of the thirty-four answered. Two envelopes came back stamped "Address Unknown." So only four women did not return the form. The overwhelming responses were appreciation and interest. Examples of comments follow:

> Since making my decision to be childless twenty-five years ago, I have read countless books and magazines that refer to us and our decision in ways that are derogatory, patronizing and/or pitying. It is refreshing and comforting to read your words, and also see you put feelings I have had for so many years and hadn't been able to discuss with anyone into concepts such as "explanatory work," "friendship wedges" and "chronological weirdness."

> I am very glad to have been part of this study and enjoyed reading about other childless women.

> Really liked the ideas and the point of view.

I'm glad someone is doing this research for the non-mothers to follow.

I'm proud to be a part of it, and remain absolutely delighted (with no "rumble" even) and I know that not having children was the best choice for us. I'd love to hear what other participants have to say.

Congrats! I'd love to read the whole project—this summary just whets my appetite for more.

Thank you for giving me a voice.

I appreciated the critical support I received from several narrators:

Your write-up intrigued me—caution—take care not to layer your work too heavily in the jargon as it will lose audience and therefore impact.

Would like to see more specifics of the diversity (as well as commonalities) of experience and interpretations by ethnicity and class.

I was pleased with the responses I received, which often included more personal sharing about being childless. If intersubjective resonance is a sufficient standard by which to measure validity, my work is indeed valid.

I want to make a brief comment about participants naming themselves. This was a good idea in principle but in my directions to participants I was too vague. I made renaming themselves an option and some women did not take it. Six women said "use my real name, no problem." I decided I was not comfortable with this, since no woman knew exactly how I was going to quote her. In these cases, I ended up assigning a name. In one case, two women chose the same first name. In this case, I used their chosen last names along with the first.

The meeting at my home was small—five women attended. I had interviewed eleven women in the greater Buffalo area—the rest lived distances away. The women who attended did not know each other. After a few formal remarks by me, women began sharing some of their stories related to childlessness. The group became more and more comfortable. Basically, we ended up laughing a great deal about our lives and experiences. I had set the dessert meeting for one and a half hours; we stayed together for three hours.

Turning my thesis into a book gave me an opportunity to rethink both the methods and substance of the work. I completed it more persuaded than ever of the utility of qualitative research and the importance of reproductive freedom.

NOTES

Preface: A Researcher's Story

1. Sandra Harding, "Introduction: Is There a Feminist Method?" in her *Feminism and Methodology* (Bloomington: University of Indiana Press, 1987), p. 9.

2. Paula Voell, "For Her It Was Love, Marriage, Family," in *The Buffalo News,* Sunday, 12 April 1987, p. 1F.

3. One notable exception is a book by Ramona T. Mercer, E. G. Nichols, and G. C. Doyle, *Transitions in a Woman's Life: Major Life Events in Developmental Context* (New York: Springer Publishing Company, 1989). The assumption that women are mothers, the general societal emphasis on motherhood, and the disregard for the lives of not–mothering women provided the impetus for their study of women's development, which traces and compares mothers and not–mothers over the life course.

4. Lillian B. Rubin, *Women of a Certain Age: The Midlife Search for Self* (New York: Harper and Row, Publishers, 1979), p. 7.

5. Judith K. Brown, *In Her Prime: A New View of Middle-Aged Women* (South Hadley, Massachusetts: Bergin & Garvey Publishers, 1985), p. 2.

6. See David Gutmann, J. Grunes, and B. Griffin, "The Clinical Psychology of Later Life: Developmental Paradigms," in Nancy Datan and N. Lohmann, eds., *Transitions of Aging* (New York: Academic Press, 1980), pp. 119–131.

7. "A constant test of perseverance" is a phrase Natalie Goldberg uses in her book, *Writing Down the Bones: Freeing the Writer Within* (Boston & London: Shambhala, 1986).

8. Carolyn G. Heilbrun, *Writing a Woman's Life* (New York: W. W. Norton and Company, 1988), p. 18.

1. The Politics of Reproductive Difference

1. See Ann Snitow, "Feminist Analyses of Motherhood," in *Encyclopedia of Childbearing: Critical Perspectives,* ed. Barbara Katz Rothman

(Phoenix: Oryx Press, 1993), pp. 145–147. Quote on p. 145.

2. My question is a variation on the question posed by Nancy D. Polikoff to the lesbian community: "Who is talking about the women who don't ever want to be mothers?" Her answer is: "No one." In *Politics of the Heart: A Lesbian Parenting Anthology,* ed. Sandra Pollack and J. Vaughan (Ithaca: Firebrand Books, 1987). I came across Polikoff's question in Ann Snitow's article, "Feminism and Motherhood: An American Reading," in *Feminist Review* 40 (Spring 1992): 32–45. See especially p. 32.

3. Rosalind Petchesky argues that at the foundation of all patriarchal ideology is the idea that "Motherhood—and indeed 'motherliness,' a *state of being* and not just a social role or relationship—is the primary purpose of a woman's life." Petchesky uses the word "maternalism" to describe this collapsing of the definitions of woman and mother. See her book, *Abortion and Woman's Choice: The State, Sexuality, and Reproductive Freedom* (Boston: Northeastern University Press, 1990), p. 344.

4. Susan Faludi catalogs the growth of pronatalism in the 1980s in her book, *Backlash: The Undeclared War Against American Women* (New York: Crown Publishers, Inc., 1991). Faludi shows that pronatalism is aimed at white, middle-class women. She contrasts the "invented" infertility crisis geared to treating white, professional women with the real and ignored infertility epidemic that exists among young black women. See pp. 27–35.

5. Snitow, "Reading."

6. See Evelyn Nakano Glenn, "Gender and the Family," in *Analyzing Gender: A Handbook of Social Science Research,* ed. Beth Hess and M. M. Ferree (Beverly Hills: Sage Publications, 1987), pp. 348–380. See especially pp. 359–362. Here, and in the next two paragraphs of my text, I adopt Glenn's history of the ideology of motherhood.

7. See Michele Hoffnung, *What's a Mother To Do? Conversations on Work and Family* (Pasadena: Trilogy Books, 1992), p. 2. See especially her first chapter, "Changing Ideas About Motherhood," pp. 1–12.

8. Hoffnung, pp. 1–2.

9. Hoffnung, p. 2.

10. Glenn, pp. 359–360.

11. Kathleen Gerson, *Hard Choices: How Women Decide about Work, Career, and Motherhood* (Berkeley: University of California Press, 1985), p. 1.

12. See Betty Friedan, *The Feminine Mystique* (New York: W. W. Norton & Company, 1963); Shirley L Radl, *Mother's Day Is Over* (New York: Charterhouse I, 1973); Jessie Bernard, *The Future of Motherhood* (New York: The Dial Press, 1974); and Adrienne Rich, *Of Woman Born* (New York: W. W. Norton & Company, 1976).

13. See Yolanda A. Patterson's introductory chapter, "'Throw Momma from the Train': American and French Views of Motherhood in the Twentieth Century," for an informative, comprehensive look at feminists on motherhood. In *Simone de Beauvoir and the Demystification of Motherhood* (Ann Arbor, UMI Press, 1989), pp. 1–40.

14. Examples of feminist work that critiqued motherhood during this period are: Shulamith Firestone, *The Dialectic of Sex* (New York: Morrow, 1970); Juliett Mitchell, *Women's Estate* (New York: Pantheon, 1971); and Adrienne Rich, *Born*.

15. This is the view of Lynn Segal, who argues her position in *Is the Future Female? Troubled Thoughts on Contemporary Feminism* (New York: Peter Bedrick Books, 1988), pp. 145–6. I have been influenced by Segal's analysis as found in her chapter, "Beauty and the Beast II: Sex, Gender and Mothering," pp. 117–161.

16. This phenomenon is discussed by Naomi Gottlieb and Marti Bombyk in their article, "Strategies for Strengthening Feminist Research," in *Affilia: Journal of Women and Social Work* 2, no. 2 (1987): 23–35.

17. This term appears frequently in "Feminist Psychology: Reclaiming Liberation," the Association for Women in Psychology's 1990 National Conference program.

18. All these theorists have written extensively. For my purposes I concentrate on the following works: Nancy Chodorow, *The Reproduction of Mothering: Psychoanalysis and the Sociology of Gender* (Berkeley: University of California Press, 1978); Carol Gilligan, *In a Different Voice: Psychological Theory and Women's Development* (Cambridge: Harvard University Press, 1982); Sara Ruddick, "Thinking about Mothering—and Putting Maternal Thinking to Use," *Women's Studies Quarterly* 11, no. 4 (1983): 4–7; and *Maternal Thinking: Toward a Politics of Peace* (Boston: Beacon Press, 1989).

19. Chodorow, *Reproduction*.

20. This assertion is made by Lynn Segal.

21. Segal, p. 135.

22. The paragraph which follows is drawn from Lillian B. Rubin's book, *Intimate Strangers: Men and Women Together* (New York: Harper and Row, 1983), pp. 48–49.

23. See Nancy Chodorow, "Oedipal Asymmetries and Heterosexual Knots," in her *Feminism and Psychoanalytic Theory* (New Haven: Yale University Press, 1989), pp. 66–78.

24. Chodorow, *Reproduction*, p. 166.

25. Chodorow, *Reproduction*, p. 48.

26. See Carol Gilligan, *Different*.

27. Gilligan, *Different*, p. 35.

28. See summary of Gilligan in Cynthia Fuchs Epstein, *Deceptive Distinctions* (New Haven: Yale University Press, 1988), pp. 76–77.

29. Epstein, *Deceptive,* p. 77.

30. See Ruddick, "Maternal Thinking," in *Feminist Studies* 6, no. 2 (Summer 1980): 342–367.

31. Jean Grimshaw, *Philosophy and Feminist Thinking* (Minneapolis: University of Minnesota Press, 1986), pp. 240–241.

32. Grimshaw, pp. 240–241.

33. See Ruddick, "Thinking about."

34. This is a point made by Linda Gordon in her article, "What's New in Women's History," in *Feminist Studies/Critical Studies,* ed. Teresa de Lauretis (Bloomington: Indiana University Press, 1986), pp. 20–30.

35. Of course, these procedures are expensive and available only to those who can afford them. While infertility most often affects working-class, African–American women and women with less than a high school education, the experience of infertility among middle-class women is most visible and most treated. See Deborah Gerson, "Infertility and the Construction of Desperation," in *Socialist Review* 89, no. 3 (1989): 45–64. See especially p. 47.

36. See Arlie Hochschild, *The Second Shift: Working Parents and the Revolution at Home* (New York: Viking, 1989), p. 1.

37. The ramifications for mothers of the "soft-focus, honey-hued symbolism surrounding moms and babies," and of the ideology that women "*can do it all,*" is expounded in Susan J. Douglas's article, "Otherhood," in *In These Times,* 20–26 Sept. 1989: 12–13. Douglas critiques the unrealistic portrayal of motherhood in the media, where mothering only enhances a woman's life and causes few ripples in her capacity to work or in her closest relationships. She argues, with emotion, that the "supermom" fantasies leave many real mothers exhausted and feeling like failures.

38. Glenn, p. 360.

39. U.S. Bureau of the Census, Current Population Reports, Series P-20, No. 436, *Fertility of American Women: June 1988* (Washington, D.C.: U. S. Government Printing Office, 1989), p. 9.

40. See Mary Jane Fine, "For More Women, Motherhood is an Option, not a Destiny," *Philadelphia Inquirer,* 4 August 1989, Sec. A, pp. 1, 6.

41. M. J. Fine, "Option," p. 6.

42. Margaret K. Ambry, "Childless Chances," *American Demographics* 14 (April 1992): 55.

43. Quoted in Barbara Kantrowitz, et al., "Three's a Crowd," *Newsweek,* 1 September 1986, pp. 68–76.

44. Of course, as Jacobson and Heaton remind us in their study of voluntary childlessness in the late 1980s, the norm in U.S. society is still to have children. Most people, female and male alike, expect and want to have children. Jacobson and Heaton disagree with the common analysis that childless rates are rising and assert that the *long-term* trend in intentional childless rates appears to be downward or stable, not upward. They believe that the strength of pronatalism is revealed in this long-term trend. See Cardell K. Jacobson and T. B. Heaton, "Voluntary Childlessness Among American Men and Women in the Late 1980's," in *Social Biology* 38, no. 1–2 (Spring–Summer 1991): 79–93.

45. For a provocative discussion of feminist goals, see Rita Gross, *Buddhism After Patriarchy: A Feminist History, Analysis and Reconstruction of Buddhism* (Albany: State University of New York, 1993). See "Appendix A: Here I Stand: Feminism As Academic Method and Social Vision," pp. 291–304. Gross argues that the elimination of all dominant/submissive relationships is not only unrealistic, it is a less radical goal than a world free from gender roles. "The issue is not abolishing hierarchy, which is impossible, but establishing *proper hierarchy* . . . It connotes the proper use of power that has been properly earned, a topic not much explored in feminist thought—a serious omission in my view. But if the essence of post-patriarchal vision is freedom from gender roles, then there is no possibility of men automatically receiving any power, prestige, influence, or position simply because of their sex. Though following this guideline would not, by itself, guarantee proper hierarchy, it would abolish the worst abuses of patriarchal power" (p. 301).

46. See Joan Scott, "Deconstructing Equality–Versus–Difference: Or, The Uses of Poststructural Theory for Feminism," in *Feminist Studies* 14, no. 1 (1988): 33–50. See p. 33.

47. See Jane Flax, *Thinking Fragments: Psychoanalysis, Feminism, and Postmodernism in the Contemporary West* (Berkeley: University of California Press, 1990), p. 188.

48. Two books that have been particularly helpful in my attempts to understand poststructuralism are: Chris Weedon, *Feminist Practice and Poststructural Theory* (New York: Basil Blackwell, 1987), and Jane Flax, *Fragments*.

49. Flax, p. 29.

50. Flax, p. 31.

51. Flax, p. 31.

52. See Mary Poovey, "Feminism and Deconstruction," in *Feminist Studies* 14, no. 1 (1988): 51–65. See p. 58.

53. Flax, p. 39.

54. Flax, p. 40.

55. Flax, p. 41.

56. These are the words of Ann Ferguson, who identifies herself with a socialist–feminist perspective. Her new theory of motherhood, sexuality, and male dominance incorporates poststructural understandings. I like the way she places equal emphasis on structural and ideological components of domination. See Ann Ferguson, *Blood At the Root: Motherhood, Sexuality and Male Dominance* (London: Pandora, 1989), p. 245.

57. J. Scott, p. 34.

58. Weedon, p. 31.

59. Weedon, p. 41.

60. Weedon, p. 79.

61. See Leslie Wahl Rabine's article, "A Feminist Politics of Non-Identity," in *Feminist Studies* 14, no. 1 (1988): 11–31. See p. 15.

62. J. Scott, p. 37.

63. Weedon, p. 23.

64. See Ellen C. Dubois, Grace P. Kelley, et al., *Feminist Scholarship: Kindling in the Groves of Academe* (Chicago: University of Illinois Press, 1985).

65. This is the phrase of Barbara DuBois in "Passionate Scholarship: Notes on Values, Knowing and Method in Feminist Social Science," in *Theories of Women's Studies,* ed. Gloria Bowles and R. D. Klein (London: Routledge and Kegan Paul, 1983), pp. 105–16. See p. 109.

66. See Biddy Martin, "Feminism, Criticism, and Foucault," in *Feminism and Foucault: Reflections on Resistance,* ed. Irene Diamond and L. Quinby (Boston: Northeastern University Press, 1988), pp. 3–19. See p. 4.

67. An elaborate discussion of my methodology can be found in the appendix. I believe that detailed explication of qualitative procedures is important for the collective process of developing and refining new research approaches.

68. See Michelle Fine, *Disruptive Voices: The Possibilities of Feminist Research* (Ann Arbor: University of Michigan Press, 1992).

69. This is a phrase used by Kennedy and Davis when discussing their construction of a lesbian community history using oral history. I appreciate the perspective they offer: "Although not believing that we can present the 'objective truth' about society in history, we do assume that some interpretations reveal more about the past and about different cultures than others, and that research should try to achieve the best approximations of 'reality.' We aim in research, analysis, and writing to find the approximate balance between recognizing that our results are constructed—that they are shaped by our own culture's questions, and our personal perspectives, as well as the consciousness and position of our narrators—while offering them as part of the historical record about the

lesbian community of the 1940's and 1950's." See Elizabeth Lapovsky Kennedy and M. D. Davis, *Boots of Leather, Slippers of Gold: The History of a Lesbian Community* (New York: Routledge, 1993), pp. 15–16.

70. See Carolyn Kay Steedman, *Landscape for a Good Woman* (New Brunswick: Rutgers University Press, 1987), p. 84.

71. See Jane English, *Childlessness Transformed: Stories of Alternative Parenting* (Mount Shasta: Earth Heart, 1989), pp. 25–37. The people English invited to contribute to her book were "childless people who have a spiritual perspective and who embody the parenting qualities of nurturing, challenging, teaching, giving commitment, taking responsibility, transmitting culture, and trusting in a positive future." The collection ends with a chapter entitled, "A Cross-Cultural and Historical Overview of the Roles of Childless People," which explores the variety of oppressions operating in different cultures as well as the contributions made by the childless.

72. See Irene Reti, ed., *Childless By Choice: A Feminist Anthology* (Santa Cruz: Herbooks, 1992).

73. Jennifer Jordan, "No Bundles of Joy," in *Essence* 21, no. 6 (October 1990): 42.

74. This point is made by Cynthia Fuchs Epstein in her article titled, "Tinkerbells and Pinups: The Construction and Reconstruction of Gender Boundaries at Work," in *Cultivating differences: symbolic boundaries and the making of inequality,* ed. Michele Lamont and M. Founier (Chicago: University of Chicago Press, 1992), pp. 232–256. See p. 252.

75. Kennedy and Davis, *Boots*.

2. Troubling Developments

1. Janice Doane and Devon Hodges, *From Klein to Kristeva: Psychoanalytic Feminism and the Search for the "Good Enough" Mother* (Ann Arbor: University of Michigan Press, 1992), p. 38.

2. I like this notion of stirring up trouble. I am indebted to Janice Doane and Devon Hodges for the phrase. See p. 4.

3. See Judith Butler, *Gender Trouble: Feminism and the Subversion of Identity* (New York and London: Routledge, 1990).

4. See Ira Progoff, *At a Journal Workshop* (New York: Dialogue House Library, 1975).

5. The books mentioned were in most cases feminist texts. For example, books authored by Simone de Beauvoir, Kate Millet, Germaine Greer, and Kathleen Berry were cited. *Science and Health with Keys to the Scripture* by Mary Baker Eddy (Boston: The First Church of Christ, Scientist, 1875) was mentioned as well.

6. See The Personal Narratives Group, ed., *Interpreting Women's Lives: Feminist Theory and Personal Narratives* (Bloomington: Indiana University Press, 1989).

7. *Narratives*, p. 5.

8. *Narratives*, p. 7.

9. *Narratives*, p. 7.

10. See Francesca M. Cancian, *Love in America: Gender and Self-Development* (New York: Cambridge University Press, 1987) for a provocative political analysis of the controversy surrounding the morality of self-development. She argues that in the past twenty-five years, self-development has been a primary goal for men and women alike. Most scholars have criticized this trend to greater independence, arguing that it promotes selfishness and undermines family bonds. Cancian disagrees. She argues instead that love and self-development do not conflict but reinforce each other.

11. I did not ask specifically about dolls, but let women talk freely about themselves as children. One wonders if such stories would have been shared if the research topic was not about childlessness and if I had concealed my own intentionally childless status.

12. Weedon, p. 77.

13. Weedon, p. 77.

14. Weedon, p. 77.

15. Carolyn Heilbrun found a similar phenomenon in the lives of women writers: "The woman who writes herself a life beyond convention . . . has usually early recognized in herself a special gift without name or definition. Its most characteristic indication is the dissatisfaction it causes her to feel with appropriate gender assignments." See Carolyn G. Heilbrun, *Writing a Woman's Life* (New York: W. W. Norton and Company, 1988), p. 96.

16. Although this chapter does not deal directly with the ways gender varies across cultures, it is important to remember that such differences do exist.

17. Research done prior to the 1970s argued that intentionally childless women were deviant, not only in terms of transgressing a specific social norm, but also in terms of their total personalities. See Sharon K. Houseknecht, "Voluntary Childlessness," in *Handbook of Marriage and the Family,* ed. M. B. Sussman and S. K. Steinmetz (New York: Plenum Press, 1987), pp. 369–95. See p. 379.

18. "Class mobility" is my language, not the language of participants. Although their words can be seen as evidence of class aspirations, women were more likely to see themselves as aspiring to "something different," and that was often defined in terms of opportunities for self-development and economic independence.

19. As might be expected, parents did not give mixed messages about the appropriateness of the heterosexual norm. One narrator recalled her father's violent reaction to her erotic attachments to other girls: "I had a lot of little problems because of my liking the little girls. You know I had a very close little girlfriend in that time that I was extremely close with, that I was in love with. And I ran into problems, probably around eleven or twelve, with liking a little Chicago cop's daughter . . . I sent her a love note. I never touched any of these kids, you know, I never had any homosexual experiences with them. But this cop came down on my father and then my father came down on me for something that I didn't really understand . . . But I can remember that was a time that my father was just violently angry and I didn't understand what was wrong. I truly didn't."

20. See Barbara Levy Simon, *Never Married Women* (Philadelphia: Temple University Press, 1987).

21. Simon, p. 7.

22. See Steedman, especially her chapter titled "Reproduction and Refusal," pp. 83–97.

23. Steedman, p. 85.

24. These stories, a reminder of the complex relations between class and gender, provide support for a particular model of the relationship between social status and fertility. Couples (and presumably individuals) with the greatest economic disadvantages are also those who must make the greatest sacrifices in order to have children. Thus those at the bottom who seek economic improvement may see a greater cost or risk to children than will those in the middle or at the top who also seek economic improvement. For a discussion of this view, with data from the baby boom generation, see Robert L. Boyd, "Childlessness and Social Mobility During the Baby Boom," in *Sociological Spectrum* 9 (1989): 425–438.

25. Federal law, from 1932 to 1937, prohibited more than one family member from working in the federal civil service. State and local governments instituted similar policies. Those policies were repeated in industry, and bias against wives was extended to the educational field and organized labor. Many women workers ended up lying about their marital status in order to get or keep jobs. See Jane Humphries, "Women: Scapegoats and Safety Valves in the Great Depression," *Review of Radical Political Economics* 8 (Spring 1976): 111.

26. See Clara Mayo, "Training for Positive Marginality," in *Applied Social Psychology Annual* (Beverly Hills: Sage Publications, 1982): 55–73.

27. See Flax, p. 166.

28. The phrase "mad to live" belongs to Jack Kerouac and refers to the Beat Generation. Liz Heron asserts that this urge is not a male

impulse alone. I like the images this phrase conjures up, and it captures in a general way the eagerness for living that many women in my sample report. See Liz Heron, *Changes of Heart: Reflections on Women's Independence* (New York: Pandora, 1986), p. 225.

29. See Michelle Stanworth, ed., *Reproductive Technologies: Gender, Motherhood and Medicine* (Minneapolis: University of Minnesota Press, 1987), p. 14.

30. Weedon, p. 130.

3. Explaining the Choice

1. David F. Noble, "Present Tense Technology: Part Three," *Democracy* 3, no. 4 (1983): 89.

2. This commentary on the word choice is drawn from Adrienne Rich in an interview published in *The American Poetry Review* (Jan.–Feb. 1991): 7–10.

3. I think Firestone overstates the situation—or do I? See Shulamith Firestone, *The Dialectic of Sex* (New York: Morrow, 1970), pp. 189–190.

4. See Charlotte Ford, "Etiquette: Doing It Right," in *McCall's* (June 1988): 97.

5. Quoted in "Review Essay" of Catharine MacKinnon's *Feminism Unmodified,* in *Off Our Backs* 17, no. 6 (1987): 13.

6. Weedon, p. 111.

7. Celia Kitzinger provides a thorough critique of the liberal humanistic construction of lesbianism as a "lifestyle," as a "choice," in her book *The Social Construction of Lesbianism* (Beverly Hills: Sage Publications, 1987). I adopt aspects of her analysis. See especially p. 34.

8. I don't mean to suggest here that if social conditions were more sympathetic, all women would choose to be mothers. Some women have no desire to parent. Even under "perfect" societal conditions, some number of women (more? fewer?) would remain childless.

9. See Tillie Olsen, "Women Who are Writers in Our Century: One Out of Twelve," in *College English* 34, no. 1 (October 1972): 6–17. Quote on p. 10.

10. These statements by women come close to the discourse of "selfishness" that is often used to discredit childlessness. It is important to remember that self-development and social power are acceptable goals for men, but since women are expected to devote themselves to others, these behaviors in women are perceived as evidence of selfishness. Women in my sample, in fact, commonly used their time, talents, and money to

advance social goals. The symbolic censure of not–mothers is fully explored in another chapter.

11. Earlier in this century, public life and domestic life for middle-class women were remarkably constrained. In *City Unions: Managing Discontent in New York City* (New Brunswick: Rutgers University Press, 1987), Mark Maier recounts that "As late as 1904 teachers were inspected visually by the superintendent to see if they were pregnant and could be suspended for 'gross misconduct' if they married" (p. 26).

12. Poet Alicia Ostriker is a persuasive proponent of the "do–both" ideology. In 1983 she wrote: "That women should have babies rather than books is the considered opinion of Western civilization. That women should have books rather than babies is a variation on that theme." For the most part, men have not been in the position where they have been forced to choose between children and other self-defining work. Yet here Ostriker assumes all women should have both. Ostriker demonstrates the overt conflict that can exist between mothers and not–mothers as she recounts the hostile reaction of "a group of students who had absorbed a certain line of militant feminist doctrine" to a poem she wrote about pregnancy and childbirth. "My suggestion to this group that motherhood for me was like sex, a peck of trouble but I wouldn't want to go through life without it, was intended to produce laughter and illumination. Instead it produced outrage. Motherhood to them was a burden imposed on women by patriarchy—which I took personally and defensively." See *Writing Like a Woman* (Ann Arbor: Univ. of Michigan Press, 1983), especially her chapter, "A Wild Surmise: Motherhood and Poetry," pp. 126–131.

13. See the following: Diana Gittins, *The Family in Question* (London: Macmillan, 1985); Kathleen Gerson, *Choices*; and Michelle Stanworth.

14. See Ann Duffy, N. Mandell, and N. Pupo, *Few Choices: Women, Work and Family* (Toronto: Garamond Press, 1989), p. 106.

15. See Karen Lindsey, "Middle-Aged, Childless, and No Regrets," *Sojourner: The Women's Forum* 12:12 (August 1987): 20–21.

16. Susan S. Lang, *Women Without Children: The Reasons, The Rewards, The Regrets* (New York: Pharos Books, 1991), p. 77.

17. Noble, p. 89.

18. Epstein, *Deceptive,* p. 201.

19. See Susan L. Williams, "Reproductive Motivations and Contemporary Feminine Development," in *The Psychology of Today's Woman: New Psychoanalytic Visions,* ed. Toni Bernay and D. W. Cantor (New York: The Analytic Press, 1986), pp. 167–193. Quote on p. 167.

20. See Berenice Fisher, "Against the Grain: Lives of Women Without Children," in *Iris* 12:2 (Spring/Summer 1992): 46–51.

21. Fisher, p. 49.

4. Symbolic Politics I

1. Segal, p. xi.

2. This is a point made by Patricia D. Spitler in her article, "Reproductive Religion," in *The Humanist* (May/June 1992): 22–23, 40.

3. This is the language of Thomas Szasz. See his *Ideology and Insanity* (London: Calder & Boyers, 1973).

4. See Jane M. Ussher, *The Psychology of the Female Body* (London: Routledge, 1989), p. 17.

5. In this history I draw on Ussher's summary of how women's reproductive capacity has been used to subordinate women, and I adapt her synopsis to emphasize the impact of this history on childless women. See Ussher, pp. 1–17.

6. Ussher, p. 2.

7. This is a quote from Barbara Ehrenreich and D. English, *For Her Own Good: 150 Years of Experts' Advice to Women* (London: Pluto Press, 1979), p. 116. Quoted in Ussher, p. 2.

8. See Ruth Hubbard, "Social Effects of Some Contemporary Myths about Women," in *Race, Class, and Gender in the United States: An Integrated Study,* 2nd Ed., ed. Paula S. Rothenberg (New York: St. Martin's Press, 1992), pp. 45–51. Quote on p. 48.

9. Ussher, p. 3.

10. Ussher, p. 5.

11. Ussher, p. 6.

12. Ussher, p. 10.

13. Of course, a further splitting occurs between good mother/bad mother. Feminists and others have reported on the conflict that may develop between stay-at-home mothers and working mothers.

14. See Grimshaw for a detailed discussion of this trend.

15. This is a phrase used in the introductory collection of essays from *Signs* on mothering and patriarchy edited by Jean F. O'Barr, D. Pope, and Mary Wyer. See *Ties That Bind* (Chicago: University of Chicago Press, 1990), p. 1.

16. Katha Pollitt uses this term in her article, "Marooned on Gilligan's Island: Are Women Morally Superior to Men?" in *The Nation* 255, no. 9 (28 December 1992): 799–807.

17. See Anita D. McClellan, "Women Who Work Too Much," in *The Women's Review of Books* IV, no. 9 (June 1987): 8–9. Quote on p. 9.

18. McClellan, p. 9.

19. O'Barr, Pope, and Wyer, p. 1.

20. Cynthia Fuchs Epstein credits the phrase "possible selves" to Hazel Markus and Paul Nurius, who wrote an article with the title "Possible

Selves" that appeared in *American Psychology* 41 (Sept. 1986): 954–969. See Epstein, "Tinkerbells," p. 234.

21. See Judy Kay, "What DINKS do: They don't have kids, but they love their lifestyles," *Niagara Gazette,* 17 November 1991, sec. E, pp. 1 and 3.

22. Kay, p. E3.

23. This stereotype of the selfish childless married woman was promoted in the nineteenth century by the American Medical Association through its anti-abortion campaign. The "selfish Aborting matron"—the bourgeois married woman who did not want to be inconvenienced by children—was contrasted with "The True Woman," who "joyfully accepted her reproductive role." Married women who aborted were labeled selfish, in part because they were seen to be risking the survival of the Anglo-Saxon race which could be overtaken by reproducing immigrants. See Carole Joffe, "Abortion and Antifeminism," in *Politics and Society* 15, no. 2 (1986–1987): 207–212. A similar argument is made by Ben Wattenberg in his book, *The Birth Dearth* (New York: Pharos Books, 1987). In his view, white, middle-class and upper middle-class educated women who marry and remain childless are not just involved in personal dramas. "They are . . . responsible for the impending population decline and political fall of the entire Western world." See Ellen Goodman's commentary, "The Birth or Time Dearth?" In *The Philadelphia Inquirer,* 4 August 1988, Sec. A, p. 11.

24. Pollitt, p. 803.

25. Pollitt, p. 803.

26. Women do remember biological relatives in their wills. Nieces and nephews were most often mentioned, along with mothers and siblings. However, women emphasized their plans for public giving.

27. Epstein, "Tinkerbells," p. 237.

28. This is a statement I adapted from Joel Kovel, who writes: "Mental illness might be a myth, but myth itself is a powerful reality." See Joel Kovel, *The Age of Desire: Reflections of a Radical Psychoanalyst* (New York: Pantheon Books, 1981), p. 34.

5. Symbolic Politics II

1. See Loraine O'Connell, "No Children, No Regrets," *The Buffalo News,* 3 February 1991.

2. See Diana Burgwyn, *Marriage Without Children* (New York: Harper and Row, 1981).

3. Jean Veevers, a Canadian sociologist, found that for some childless women, taking on the care of a pet is seen as undesirable. [See Jean

Veevers, "The Life Style of Voluntarily Childless Couples," in *The Canadian Family in Comparative Perspective* (Ontario: Prentice Hall of Canada, 1976), p. 403.] Randee Bloom Johnson suggests lack of interest may imply "a major narcissistic issue as a possible motivation for childlessness . . . the perception of the pet as interfering with the adult life style points to a particular difficulty in focusing energy on anything beyond one's immediate self." This kind of psychological analysis is part of the problem childless women confront. See Randee Bloom Johnson, "Psychodynamic and Developmental Considerations of Childless Older Women," Diss., Northwestern Univ., 1981, p. 23.

4. Rom Harré, ed., *The Social Construction of Emotions* (New York: Basil Blackwell, Inc., 1986).

5. See Claire Armon-Jones, "The Social Functions of Emotion," in *The Social Construction of Emotions,* ed. Rom Harre (New York: Basil Blackwell Inc., 1986), pp. 57–82.

6. Harre, pp. 4–5.

7. Maxine Paetro, *Baby-Dreams* (New York: Simon and Schuster, 1989). On p. 302, the novelist writes about a woman who desperately wants a baby with a man who doesn't: "How could she have asked him to change everything about his own experience—snap, like that—because she had become panicked and frightened of being childless?"

8. See Sharon K. Houseknecht, "Reference Group Support for Voluntary Childlessness: Evidence for Conformity" in *Journal of Marriage and the Family* 39 (1977): 285–292.

9. See "Oh Dear, I Forgot to Have Children," in *Off Our Backs* (May 1992): 17.

10. Irena Klepfisz speaks movingly about the fantasy that a child will save you from isolation and loneliness. See "Women Without Children/Women Without Families/Women Alone," in *Dreams of an Insomniac: Feminist Essays, Speeches, and Diatribes* (Portland, Or: Eighth Mountain Press, 1990), p. 63. Klepfisz is one of the women interviewed in Lang's *Women Without Children.* See Lang, pp. 168–169.

11. See Baine B. Alexander, R. L. Rubinstein, M. Goodman, and M. Luborsky, "A Path Not Taken: A Cultural Analysis of Regrets and Childlessness in the Lives of Older Women," *The Gerontologist* 32, no. 5 (1992): 618–626.

12. Alexander et al., p. 626.

13. Alexander et al., p. 624.

14. See Katie Kroneberg, "Am I the Only Woman Who Regrets Having Children?" *Off Our Backs* 22, no. 9 (Aug./Sept. 1992): 17–18.

15. See Epstein, "Tinkerbells," p. 232.

16. See Hubbard in Rothenberg, p. 45.

6. The Social World of Childless Women

1. Poovey, pp. 58–59.

2. This is a phrase used by Francesca M. Cancian in *Love in America: Gender and Self-Development* (New York: Cambridge University Press, 1987), which nicely characterizes how women in my sample, as a whole, felt about their relationships.

3. See Susan S. Lang, *Women Without Children: The Reasons, The Rewards, The Regrets* (New York: Pharos Books, 1991), p. 222.

4. See a review of Haskell's book, *Love and Other Infectious Diseases,* by Delia Ephron, "Too Close for Comfort," in *The New York Times Book Review,* 8 April 1990, p. 9.

5. See Diane Ehrensaft, *Parenting Together: Men and Women Sharing the Care of Children* (New York: Free Press, 1987).

6. See Ann Oakley, *Taking It Like a Woman: A Personal History* (New York: Random House, 1984), p. 126.

7. See Diana Gittins, *The Family in Question: Changing Household and Familiar Ideologies* (London: Macmillan, 1985), p. 162. Gittins is a British sociologist but the point she makes holds true in the United States.

8. Simon, p. 97.

9. I appreciate the research done by Timothy Brubaker, who controls for parenthood in his study, *Later Life Families* (Beverly Hills: Sage Publications, 1985), pp. 62–64.

10. This is a point made by Berenice Fisher in her excellent article.

11. See Patricia Hill Collins, "On Our Own Terms: Self-Defined Standpoints and Curriculum Transformation," in *NWSA Journal* 3, no. 3 (Autumn 1991): 367–381.

12. Fisher, p. 50.

13. Fisher, p. 50.

14. See bell hooks, *Feminist Theory: from margin to center* (Boston: South End Press, 1984), pp. 133–146. Quote on pp. 141–142.

15. See Christine Overall, *Ethics and Human Reproduction: A Feminist Analysis* (Boston: Unwin Hyman, 1987), pp. 144–145.

16. Overall, p. 145.

17. See Susan Shapiro, "Motherhood and Friendship," in *Sojourner: The Women's Forum* (August 1987): 18–19.

18. Shapiro, p. 18.

19. Heron, p. 183.

20. Deborah Heiligman, "Us and Them," *Parents* (June 1990): 101–102.

21. Heiligman, p. 102.

22. Collins, "Terms," p. 373.

23. Heilbrun, p. 97.

24. See Juliet B. Schor, *The Overworked American: The Unexpected Decline of Leisure* (New York: Basic Books, 1991).

25. See Marilyn Gardner in an article titled, "Derailed on the 'Daughter Track,'" in *The Christian Science Monitor*, 20 June 1989, p. 14. This article asserts that elder care promises to be an "emerging employee benefit of the 1990's." But is it really a benefit? For instance, "at AT&T, a new labor contract is being hailed as a 'breakthrough' in employee benefits. In addition to provisions for child care, the package allows employees to take up to one year of unpaid leave to care for ailing relatives." This probably means that individual women will continue to provide the socially necessary work of caretaking in isolating conditions without pay.

26. Gardner.

27. Gardner.

7. Conclusion

1. Ellen Herman, "Still Married After All These Years?" In *Sojourner: The Women's Forum* (September 1990): 14S–15S.

2. Ferguson, p. 81.

3. Kathleen Gerson, "Emerging Social Divisions Among Women: Implications for Welfare State Politics," *Politics and Society* 15, no. 2 (1986–87): 213–214.

4. Given changing demographic patterns, care in later life is an issue that mothers and nonmothers can unite around. Mothers now in their fifties may find no one to take care of them when they become elderly, according to a note titled "Daughter Shortage" in *American Demographics* 8, no. 5 (1986): 13–14. Since 1990 most middle-aged women are in the work force, making it unlikely that they are available to care for elderly mothers. The note concludes: "A few years ago, a feminist rallying cry was, 'I need a wife;' in the years ahead, feminists may be crying, 'I need a daughter.'"

5. These words of Susan Bordo appear in her essay, "The Body and the Reproduction of Femininity: A Feminist Appropriation of Foucault," in *Gender/Body/Knowledge: Feminist Reconstructions of Being and Knowing*, ed. Alison M. Jaggar and Susan R. Bordo (New Brunswick: Rutgers University Press, 1989), pp. 13–33.

6. Ann Duffy, Nancy Mandell, and Norene Pupo, *Few Choices: Women, Work and Family* (Toronto: Garamond Press, 1989), p. 105.

7. Duffy et al., p. 105.

8. For in-depth analyses of the conflicts between feminist mothering theories and Foucaultian discourse, see the debate between Isaac D. Balbus ("Disciplining Women: Michel Foucault and the Power of Feminist Discourse") and Jana Sawicki ("Feminism and the Power of Foucaultian Discourse") in *After Foucault: Humanistic Knowledge, Postmodern Challenges,* ed. Jonathan Arac (New Brunswick: Rutgers University Press, 1988), pp. 138–178.

9. Poovey, p. 55.

10. Gerson, *Choices,* p. 4.

11. Poovey, p. 52.

12. See Barbara Katz Rothman, *Recreating Motherhood: Ideology and Technology in a Patriarchal Society* (New York: W. W. Norton, 1989), p. 19.

13. Rothman, p. 23.

14. bell hooks, *Sisters of the Yam: black women and self-recovery* (Boston: South End Press, 1993), p. 171.

15. Snitow, "Reading," p. 42.

16. See Gittins, p. 110.

17. M. Elizabeth Tidball reminds us of the connection between women's nonbiological competence and women's liberation. See her article, "On Liberation and Competence," in *The Educational Record* 57, no. 2 (1976): 101–110.

18. Tidball, p. 104.

19. Tidball, p. 105.

Appendix: About the Research

1. Flax, *Fragments,* p. 223.

2. See Patrick Biernacki and Dan Waldorf, "Snowball Sampling: Problems and Techniques of Chain Referral Sampling," *Sociological Methods and Research* 10, no. 2 (1981): 141–163.

3. Lillian Rubin, *Women of a Certain Age: The Midlife Search for Self* (New York: Harper and Row, 1979), pp. 214–225.

4. Pamela Daniels and Kathy Weingarten, *Sooner or Later: The Timing of Parenthood in Adult Lives* (New York: W. W. Norton and Company, 1983), pp. 305–322.

5. See E. Krausz, "Psychology and Race," *Race* 10 (1969): 361–368.

6. I did receive one refusal of assistance from the administrator of an expensive retirement home. In a letter of response to my letter asking for help in identifying potential participants she wrote:

I must refuse your request since our ladies no.1—Do not qualify for the age ranges you have outlined and no. 2—they would not wish to take part in a survey or study which necessitated them discussing personal preferences or choices in their lives. They are from a very different time frame where one did not discuss their personal lives.

7. See The Personal Narratives Group, *Interpreting Women's Lives: Feminist Theory and Personal Narratives* (Bloomington: Indiana University Press, 1989), p. 4.

8. Ira Progoff, *At a Journal Workshop* (New York: Dialogue House Library, 1975), p. 109.

9. See Ann Oakley, "Interviewing Women: A Contradiction in Terms?" in *Doing Feminist Research,* ed. H. Roberts (London: Routledge and Kegan Paul, 1981).

10. These books and articles included the works of Weedon, Flax, Rabine, Scott, Poovey, Martin, Grimshaw, and Segal.

11. See Rubin, *Midlife,* pp. 214–225.

12. Rubin, *Midlife,* p. 223.

13. See Tristine Rainer, *The New Diary: How to Use a Journal for Self-Guidance and Expanded Creativity* (Los Angeles: Jeremy P. Tarcher, Inc., 1978), p. 34.

14. See Biddy Martin, "Feminism, Criticism, and Foucault," in *Feminism and Foucault: Reflections on Resistance,* ed. Irene Diamond and L. Quinby (Boston: Northeastern University Press, 1988), p. 18.

15. Martin, p. 103.

16. See Kathleen Gerson, *Hard Choices: How Women Decide about Work, Career, and Motherhood* (Berkeley: University of California Press, 1985), p. 33.

17. This is a question that Celia Kitzinger asks in *Construction,* p. 189.

18. Kitzinger, p. 189.

19. Bohan, p. 13.

BIBLIOGRAPHY

Alexander, Baine B., R. L. Rubinstein, et al. "A Path Not Taken: A Cultural Analysis of Regrets and Childlessness in the Lives of Older Women." In *The Gerontologist* 32, no. 5 (1992): 618–626.

Ambry, Margaret K. "Childless Chances." In *American Demographics* 14 (April 1992): 55.

Arac, Jonathan, ed. *After Foucault: Humanistic Knowledge, Postmodern Challenges.* New Brunswick: Rutgers Univ. Press, 1988.

Association of Women in Psychology. "Feminist Psychology: Reclaiming Liberation." National Conference Program, Tempe, Arizona, 8–11 March 1988.

Bachrach, Christine. "Childlessness and Social Isolation Among the Elderly." In *Journal of Marriage and the Family* (August 1980): 627–36.

Baruch, Grace R., et al. *Lifeprints: New Patterns of Love and Work for Today's Woman.* New York: McGraw Hill, 1983.

Beckman, L. J., and B. B. Houser. "The Consequences of Childlessness on the Social-Psychological Well-Being of Older Women." In *Journal of Gerontology* 37 (1982): 243–50.

Bernard, Jessie. *The Future of Motherhood.* New York: The Dial Press, 1974.

Bernay, Toni, and D. W. Cantor, eds. *The Psychology of Today's Woman: New Psychoanalytic Visions.* New York: The Analytic Press, 1986.

Biernacki, Patrick, and D. Waldorf. "Snowball Sampling: Problems and Techniques of Chain Referral Sampling." In *Sociological Methods and Research* 10, no. 2 (1981): 141–63.

Blake, J. "Is Zero Preferred? American Attitudes Toward Childlessness in the 1970's." *Journal of Marriage and the Family* 41 (1979): 245–57.

Bloom, David, and N. Bennett. "Childless Couples." In *American Demographics* (August 1986).

Bohan, Janis S. "Regarding Gender: Essentialism, Constructionism, and Feminist Psychology." In *Psychology of Women Quarterly* 17 (1993): 5–21.

Boyd, Robert L. "Racial Differences in Childlessness: A Centennial Review." In *Sociological Perspectives* 32, no. 2 (1989): 183–99.

Bram, S. "To Have or Have Not: A Social Psychological Study of Voluntary Childless Couples, Parents-to-Be, and Parents." Diss., Univ. of Michigan, Ann Arbor, 1974.

Brown, Judith K. *In Her Prime: A New View of Middle-Aged Women*. South Hadley, Massachusetts: Bergin and Garvey Publishers, Inc., 1985.

Brubaker, Timothy. *Later Life Families*. Beverly Hills: Sage Publications, 1985.

Burgwyn, Diana. *Marriage Without Children*. New York: Harper and Row, 1981.

Burnside, B. "Gender Roles and Lifestyle: A Sociocultural Study of Voluntary Childlessness." Diss., Univ. of Washington, Seattle, 1977.

Butler, Judith. *Gender Trouble: Feminism and the Subversion of Identity*. New York: Routledge, 1990.

Callan, V. J. "Perceptions of Parents, the Voluntarily and the Involuntarily Childless: A Multidimensional Scaling Analysis." In *Journal of Marriage and The Family* 47 (1985): 1045–50.

Campbell, A., P. Converse, and W. Rodgers. *The Quality of American Life*. New York: Russell Sage Foundation, 1976.

Campbell, Elaine. *The Childless Marriage: An Exploratory Study of Couples Who Do Not Want Children*. London and New York: Tavistock, 1985.

Cancian, Francesca M. *Love in America: Gender and Self-Development*. New York: Cambridge Univ. Press, 1987.

Chodorow, Nancy. "Oedipal Asymmetries and Heterosexual Knots." In her *Feminism and Psychoanalytic Theory*. New Haven: Yale Univ. Press, 1989.

———. *The Reproduction of Mothering: Psychoanalysis and the Sociology of Gender*. Berkeley: Univ. of California Press, 1978.

Collins, Patricia Hill. "On Our Own Terms: Self-Defined Standpoints and Curriculum Transformation." In *NWSA Journal* 3, no. 3 (Autumn 1991): 367–381.

Creager, Ellen. "On Issue of Work, It's Mom vs. Mom." In *Buffalo News*. 20 Sept. 1989, Sec. B., p. 7.

Daniels, Pamela, and K. Weingarten. *Sooner or Later: The Timing of Parenthood in Adult Lives*. New York: W. W. Norton, 1983.

"Daughter Shortage." In *American Demographics* 8, no. 5 (1986): 13–14.

de Lauretis, Teresa, ed. *Feminist Studies/Critical Studies*. Bloomington: Indiana University Press, 1986.

Diamond, Irene, and L. Quinby, eds. *Feminism and Foucault: Reflections on Resistance*. Boston: Northeastern University Press, 1988.

Dietz, T. "Factors Influencing Childlessness Among American Women." Diss., Univ. of California, Davis, 1979.

Doane, Janice, and D. Hodges. *From Klein to Kristeva: Pyschoanalytic Feminism and the Search for the "Good Enough" Mother.* Ann Arbor: University of Michigan Press, 1992.

Douglas, Carol Anne. "Oh Dear, I Forgot To Have Children!" In *Off Our Backs* 22, no. 5 (May 1992): 17.

Douglas, Susan J. "Otherhood." In *In These Times,* 20–26 Sept. 1989, pp. 12–13.

Dubois, Ellen C., and G. P. Kelley, et al. *Feminist Scholarship: Kindling in the Groves of Academe.* Chicago: Univ. of Illinois Press, 1985.

DuBois, Barbara. "Passionate Scholarship: Notes on Values, Knowing and Method in Feminist Social Science." In *Theories of Women's Studies,* ed. Gloria Bowles and R. D. Klein. London: Routledge and Kegan Paul, 1983.

Duffy, Ann, and N. Mandell, et al. *Few Choices: Women Work and Family.* Toronto: Garamond Press, 1989.

Eddy, Mary Baker. *Science and Health with Keys to the Scripture.* Boston: The First Church of Christ, Scientist, 1875.

Ehrensaft, Diane. *Parenting Together: Men and Women Sharing the Care of Their Children.* New York: Free Press, 1987.

Eisenstein, Zillah R. *The Female Body and the Law.* Berkeley: Univ. of California Press, 1988.

English, Jane. *Childlessness Transformed: Stories of Alternative Parenting.* Mount Shasta: Earth Heart, 1989.

Ephron, Delia. "Too Close for Comfort." In *The New York Times Book Review,* 8 April 1990, p. 9.

Epstein, Cynthia Fuchs. *Deceptive Distinctions.* New Haven, Yale Univ. Press, 1988.

Faludi, Susan. *Backlash: The Undeclared War Against American Women.* New York: Crown Publishers, 1991.

Faux, Marian. *Childless by Choice: Choosing Childlessness in the 80's.* Garden City: Anchor Press/Doubleday, 1984.

Ferguson, Ann. *Blood At the Root: Motherhood, Sexuality and Male Dominance.* London: Pandora, 1989.

Fine, Mary Jane. "For More Women, Motherhood is an Option, Not a Destiny." In *Philadelphia Inquirer,* 4 Aug. 1989, Sec. A, pp. 1, 6.

Fine, Michelle. *Disruptive Voices: The Possibilities of Feminist Research.* Ann Arbor: University of Michigan Press, 1992.

Firestone, Shulamith. *The Dialectic of Sex.* New York: Morrow, 1970.

Fisher, Berenice. "Against The Grain: Lives of Women Without Children." In *Iris* 12, no. 2 (Spring/Summer 1992).

Flax, Jane. *Thinking Fragments: Psychoanalysis, Feminism, and Postmodernism in the Contemporary West.* Berkeley: Univ. of California Press, 1990.

Flodin, Kim C. "Starting a Family Later is Passe, a Fad of the 70's." In *The Buffalo News,* 9 Nov. 1989, Sec. B., p. 3.

Ford, Charlotte. "Etiquette: Doing It Right." In *McCall's* (June 1988): 97.

Friedan, Betty. *The Feminine Mystique.* New York: W. W. Norton & Company, 1963.

Gardner, Marilyn. "Derailed on the 'Daughter Track.'" In *The Christian Science Monitor,* 20 June 1989, p. 14.

Gerson, Deborah. "Infertility and the Construction of Desperation." In *Socialist Review* 89, no. 3 (1989): 45–64.

Gerson, Kathleen. "Emerging Social Divisions Among Women: Implications for Welfare State Politics." In *Politics and Society* 15, no. 2 (1986–87): 213–14.

———. *Hard Choices: How Women Decide about Work, Career, and Motherhood.* Berkeley: Univ. of California Press, 1985.

Gilligan, Carol. *In a Different Voice: Psychological Theory and Women's Development.* Cambridge: Harvard Univ. Press, 1982.

Gittins, Diana. *The Family in Question: Changing Household and Familiar Ideologies.* London: Macmillan, 1985.

Glenn, Evelyn N. "Gender and the Family." In *Analyzing Gender: A Handbook of Social Science Research,* ed. Beth Hess and M. M. Ferree. Beverly Hills: Sage Publications, 1987.

Goldberg, Natalie. *Writing Down the Bones: Freeing the Writer Within.* Boston: Shambhala, 1986.

Goodman, Ellen. "The Birth or Time Dearth?" In *The Philadelphia Inquirer,* 4 August 1988, Sec. A., p. 11.

Gordon, Linda. "What's New in Women's History?" In *Feminist Studies/Critical Studies,* ed. Teresa de Lauretis. Bloomington: Indiana University Press, 1986, 20–30.

Gottlieb, Naomi, and M. Bombyk. "Strategies for Strengthening Feminist Research." In *Affilia: Journal of Women and Social Work* 2, no. 2 (1987): 23–35.

Grimshaw, Jean. *Philosophy and Feminist Thinking.* Minneapolis: Univ. of Minnesota Press, 1986.

Gross, Rita. *Buddhism After Patriarchy: A Feminist History, Analysis and Reconstruction of Buddhism.* Albany: State University of New York, 1993.

Gutmann, David, J. Grunes, and B. Griffin. "The Clinical Psychology of Later Life: Developmental Paradigms." In *Transitions of Aging,* ed. Nancy Datan and N. Lohmann. New York: Academic Press, 1980, pp. 119–31.

Hacker, Andrew. "Women at Work." In *The New York Review of Books* 33, no. 13 (1986): 26–32.

Harding, Sandra. "Introduction: Is There a Feminist Method?" In her *Feminism and Methodology.* Bloomington: Univ. of Indiana Press, 1987.

Harré, Rom, ed. *The Social Construction of Emotions*. New York: Basil Blackwell, Inc., 1986.

Harrison, Bennett, and B. Bluestone. *The Great U-Turn*. New York: Basic Books, 1988.

Heilbrun, Carolyn G. *Writing a Woman's Life*. New York: W. W. Norton, 1988.

Heiligman, Deborah. "Us and Them." *Parents* (June 1990): 101–102.

Herman, Ellen. "Still Married After All These Years?" In *Sojourner: The Women's Forum* (September 1990): 14S–15S.

Heron, Liz. *Changes of Heart: Reflections on Women's Independence*. London: Pandora Press, 1986.

Hochschild, Arlie. *The Second Shift: Working Parents and the Revolution at Home*. New York: Viking, 1989.

Hoffnung, Michele. *What's a Mother To Do? Conversations on Work and Family*. Pasadena: Trilogy Books, 1992.

hooks, bell. *Feminist Theory: from margin to center*. Boston: South End Press, 1984.

———. *Sisters of the Yam: black women and self-recovery*. Boston: South End Press, 1993.

Hotz, J. N. "An Investigation of the Nature and Defense of Voluntary Childlessness." Unpublished manuscript, Douglass College, 1975.

Houseknecht, Sharon K. "Childlessness and Marital Adjustment." In *Journal of Marriage and the Family* 41 (1979): 259–65.

———. "Reference Group Support for Voluntary Childlessness: Evidence for Conformity." In *Journal of Marriage and the Family* 39 (1977): 285–92.

———. "Voluntary Childlessness." In *Handbook of Marriage and the Family*, ed. M. B. Sussman and S. K. Steinmetz. New York: Plenum Press, 1987, pp. 369–95.

Houser, B. B., et al. "The Relative Rewards and Costs of Childlessness for Old Women." In *Psychology of Women Quarterly* 8 (1984): 395–98.

Humphries, Jane. "Women: Scapegoats and Safety Valves in the Great Depression." In *Review of Radical Political Economics* 8 (Spring 1976).

Inazu, J. K. "Perceptions of the Effects of a Newcomer as a Factor in Voluntary Childlessness." Diss., Univ. of Cincinnati, 1979.

Jacobson, Cardell K., and T. B. Heaton. "Voluntary Childlessness Among American Men and Women in the Late 1980's." In *Social Biology* 38, no. 1–2 (Spring–Summer 1991): 79–83.

Jaggar, Alison M., and S. R. Bordo, eds. *Gender/Body/Knowledge: Feminist Reconstructions of Being and Knowing*. New Brunswick: Rutgers University Press, 1989.

Jamison, P. H., et al. "Some Assumed Characteristics of Voluntarily Childfree Women and Men." In *Psychology of Women Quarterly* 4 (1979): 266–73.

Joffe, Carole. "Abortion and Antifeminism." In *Politics and Society* 15, no. 2 (1986–1987): 207–12.

Johnson, C. L., and D. J. Catalano. "Childless Elderly and Their Family Supports." In *The Gerontologist* 21, no. 6 (1981): 610–18.

Johnson, Randee B. "Psychodynamic and Developmental Considerations of Childless Older Women." Diss., Northwestern Univ., 1981.

Jones, S. H. "Toward a Psychological Profile of Childfree Women." Diss., California School of Professional Psychology, 1978.

Jordon, Jennifer. "No Bundles of Joy." In *Essence* 21, no. 6 (October 1990).

Kantrowitz, Barbara, et al. "Three's a Crowd." *Newsweek,* 1 Sept. 1986, pp. 68–76.

Kay, Judy. "What DINKS do: They don't have kids, but they love their lifestyles." *Niagara Gazette,* 17 November 1991, sec. E, pp. 1, 3.

Kennedy, Elizabeth L., and M. D. Davis. *Boots of Leather, Slippers of Gold: The History of a Lesbian Community.* New York: Routledge, 1993.

Kitzinger, Celia. *The Social Construction of Lesbianism.* Beverly Hills: Sage Publications, 1987.

Klein, Ethel. *Gender Politics.* Cambridge: Harvard Univ. Press, 1984.

Klepfisz, Irena. "Women Without Children/Women Without Families/Women Alone." In *Dreams of an Insomniac: Feminist Essays, Speeches, and Diatribes.* Portland, Or: Eighth Mountain Press, 1990.

Kovel, Joel. *The Age of Desire: Reflections of a Radical Psychoanalyst.* New York: Pantheon, 1981.

Kraith, Theresa. "Comparisons of Selected Personality Characteristics in Voluntarily Childless Women and Women Who Desire Children." Diss., California School of Professional Psychology, 1982.

Kramarae, Cheris, and P. A. Treichler, eds. *A Feminist Dictionary.* Boston: Pandora, 1985.

Krausz, E. "Psychology and Race." In *Race* 10 (1969): 361–68.

Kroneberg, Katie. "Am I the Only Woman Who Regrets Having Children?" In *Off Our Backs* 22, no. 9 (Aug/Sept 1992): 17–18.

Lamont, Michele, and M. Founier, eds. *Cultivating differences: symbolic boundaries and the making of inequality.* Chicago: University of Chicago Press, 1992.

Lang, Susan S. *Women Without Children: The Reasons, The Rewards, The Regrets.* New York: Pharos Books, 1991.

Levine, J. O. "Voluntarily Childfree Women and Mothers: A Comparative Study." *Dissertation Abstracts* 39 (1979): 3524.

Maier, Mark. *City Unions: Managing Discontent in New York City.* New Brunswick: Rutgers University Press, 1987.

Marcks, B. R. "Voluntary Childless Couples: An Exploratory Study." Unpublished master's thesis, Syracuse University, 1976.

Mayo, Clara. "Training for Positive Marginality." In *Applied Social Psychology Annual*. Beverly Hills: Sage Publications, 1982, pp. 55–73.

McBroom, Patricia A. *The Third Sex: The New Professional Woman*. New York: Morrow, 1986.

McClellan, Anita D. "Women Who Work Too Much." In *The Women's Review of Books* 4, no. 9 (June 1987): 8–9.

Mercer, Ramona T., et al. *Transitions in a Woman's Life: Major Life Events in Developmental Context*. New York: Springer Publishing Co., 1989.

Mitchell, Juliett. *Women's Estate*. New York: Pantheon, 1971.

Morell, Carolyn. "Choosing Deviance: An Examination of Childlessness by Choice." Unpublished manuscript, Univ. of Pennsylvania, 1984.

Nason, E. M., and M. M. Poloma. *Voluntary Childless Couples: The Emergence of a Variant Lifestyle*. Beverly Hills: Sage Publications, 1976.

Noble, David F. "Present Tense Technology: Part Three." In *Democracy* 3, no. 4 (1983): 71–93.

Oakley, Ann. "Interviewing Women: A Contradiction in Terms?" In *Doing Feminist Research,* ed. H. Roberts. London: Routledge and Kegan Paul, 1981.

———. *Taking It Like a Woman: A Personal History*. New York: Random House, 1984.

O'Barr, Jean F., D. Pope, and M. Wyer, eds. *Ties That Bind*. Chicago: University of Chicago Press, 1990.

O'Connell, Loraine. "No Children, No Regrets." *The Buffalo News,* 3 February 1991.

Olsen, Tillie. "Women Who are Writers in Our Century: One Out of Twelve." In *College English* 34, no. 1 (October 1972): 6–17.

Ory, M. "The Decision to Parent or Not: Normative and Structural Components." Diss., Purdue Univ., 1976.

Ostriker, Alicia. *Writing Like a Woman*. Ann Arbor: Univ. of Michigan Press, 1983.

Overall, Christine. *Ethics and Human Reproduction: A Feminist Analysis*. Boston: Unwin Hyman, 1987.

Paetro, Maxine. *Baby-Dreams*. New York: Simon and Schuster, 1989.

Patterson, Yolanda A. *Simone de Beauvoir and the Demystification of Motherhood*. Ann Arbor: UMI Press, 1989.

Peck, Ellen, and J. Sanderowitz, eds. *Pronatalism*. New York: Thomas Y. Cromwell, 1974.

Perlman, Helen H. *Persona: Social Role and Personality*. Chicago: University of Chicago Press, 1968.

Personal Narratives Group. *Interpreting Women's Lives: Feminist Theory and Personal Narratives*. Bloomington: Indiana Univ. Press, 1989.

Petchesky, Rosalind. *Abortion and Woman's Choice: The State, Sexuality, and Reproductive Freedom*. Boston: Northeastern University Press, 1990.

Polit, D. "Stereotypes Relating to Family Size Status." In *Journal of Marriage and the Family* 40, no. 1 (1978): 105–16.

Pollack, Sandra, and J. Vaughan, eds. *The Politics of the Heart: A Lesbian Parenting Anthology*. Ithaca: Firebrand Books, 1987.

Pollitt, Katha. "Marooned on Gilligan's Island: Are Women Morally Superior to Men?" *The Nation* 255, no. 9 (28 December 1992): 799–807.

Polonko, K. A. "A Comparison of the Patterns Associated with Voluntary Childlessness and Low Birth Intentions." American Sociological Association, San Francisco, Sept. 1978.

Poovey, Mary. "Feminism and Deconstruction." In *Feminist Studies* 14, no. 1 (1988): 51–65.

Progoff, Ira. *At a Journal Workshop*. New York: Dialogue House Library, 1975.

Pupo, A. M. "A Study of Childless Couples." Diss., United States International University, 1980.

Rabine, Leslie Wahl. "A Feminist Politics of Non-Identity." In *Feminist Studies* 14, no. 1 (1988): 11–31.

Radl, Shirley L. *Mother's Day Is Over*. New York: Charterhouse I, 1973.

Rainer, Tristine. *The New Diary: How to Use a Journal for Self-Guidance and Expanded Creativity*. Los Angeles: Jeremy P. Tarcher, Inc., 1978.

Rempel, J. "Childless Elderly: What Are They Missing?" *Journal of Marriage and the Family* 47 (1985): 343–48.

Reti, Irene, ed. *Childless By Choice: A Feminist Anthology*. Santa Cruz: Herbooks, 1992.

"Review Essay: Catharine MacKinnon's *Feminism Unmodified*." In *Off Our Backs* 17, no. 6 (1987): 13.

Rich, Adrienne. Interview in *The American Poetry Review* (Jan.–Feb. 1991): 7–10.

———. *Of Woman Born: Motherhood as Experience and Institution*. New York: W. W. Norton, 1976.

Rothenberg, Paula S., ed. *Race, Class, and Gender in the United States: An Integrated Study*, 2nd Ed. New York: St. Martin's Press, 1992.

Rothman, Barbara Katz. *Encyclopedia of Childbearing: Critical Perspectives*. Phoenix: Oryx, 1993.

———. *Recreating Motherhood: Ideology and Technology in a Patriarchal Society*. New York: W. W. Norton, 1989.

Rubin, Lillian. *Intimate Strangers: Men and Women Together*. New York: Harper and Row, 1983.

———. *Women of a Certain Age: The Midlife Search for Self*. New York: Harper and Row, 1979.

Rubinstein, Robert L. "Childless Elderly: Theoretical Perspectives and Practical Concerns." In *Journal of Cross-Cultural Gerontology* 2 (1987): 1–14.

Ruddick, Sara. "Maternal Thinking." In *Feminist Studies* 6, no. 2 (Summer 1980): 342–367.

———. *Maternal Thinking: Toward a Politics of Peace*. Boston: Beacon Press, 1989.

———. "Thinking about Mothering—and Putting Maternal Thinking to Use." In *Women's Studies Quarterly* 11, no. 4 (1983): 4–7.

Sapienza, Barbara G. "Reproductive Choice and Ego Development in Women aged 35–50." Diss., Pacific Graduate School of Psychology, 1987.

Scott, Joan W. "Deconstructing Equality–Versus–Difference: Or, the Uses of Poststructural Theory for Feminism." In *Feminist Studies* 14, no. 1 (1988): 33–50.

Scott, L. "Intentionally Childless Women: An Exploration of Psychosocial Factors." Unpublished manuscript, Fielding Institute, 1979.

Segal, Lynn. *Is the Future Female? Troubled Thoughts on Contemporary Feminism*. New York: Bedrick Books, 1988.

Shapiro, Susan. "Motherhood and Friendship." In *Sojourner: The Women's Forum* (August 1987): 18–19.

Sheridan, Mary B. "Pope Rules Out Priesthood for Women." In *Buffalo Evening News,* 1 Oct. 1988, Sec. A, pp. 1, 4.

Shotter, John, and K. J. Gergen, eds. *Texts of Identity*. Newbury Park, CA: Sage Publications, 1989.

Silka, L., and S. Kiesler. "Couples Who Choose to Remain Childless." In *Family Planning Perspectives* 9 (1977): 6–25.

Simon, Barbara Levy. *Never Married Women*. Philadelphia: Temple Univ. Press, 1987.

Smilgis, Martha. "Here Come the Dinks." *Time Magazine,* 20 April 1987, p. 75.

Snitow, Ann. "Feminism and Motherhood: An American Reading." In *Feminist Review* 40 (Spring 1992): 32–45.

Spitler, Patricia. "Reproductive Religion." In *The Humanist* (May/June 1992): 22–40.

Stanworth, Michelle, ed. *Reproductive Technologies: Gender, Motherhood and Medicine*. Minneapolis: Univ. of Minnesota Press, 1987.

Steedman, Carolyn Kay. *Landscape for a Good Woman*. New Brunswick: Rutgers Univ. Press, 1987.

Stimpson, Catherine. "The New Scholarship About Women: The State of the Art." CUNY Graduate Center, New York, 8 October 1980.

Stokes, S. C., and N. E. Johnson. "Birth Order, Size of Family of Orientation, and Desired Family Size." In *Journal of Individual Psychology* 33, no. 1 (1977): 42–46.

Szasz, Thomas. *Ideology and Insanity.* London: Calder & Boyers, 1973.

Teicholz, Judith G. "A Preliminary Search for Psychological Correlates of Voluntary Childlessness in Married Women." Diss., Boston Univ. School of Education, 1977.

———. "Psychological Correlates of Voluntary Childlessness in Married Women." Eastern Psychological Association, Washington, D.C., March–April 1978.

Thoen, G. A. "Commitment Among Voluntary Childfree Couples to a Variant Lifestyle." Diss., Univ. of Minnesota, Minneapolis, 1977.

Tidball, M. Elizabeth. "On Liberation and Competence." In *The Educational Record* 57, no. 2 (1976): 101–110.

Toomey, B. G. "College Women and Voluntary Childlessness: A Comparative Study of Women Indicating They Want to Have Children and Those Indicating They Do Not Want to Have Children." Diss., Ohio State Univ., 1977.

U.S. Bureau of the Census, Current Population Reports, Series P-20, No. 436. *Fertility of American Women: June 1988.* Washington, D. C.: U.S. Government Printing Office, 1989.

Ussher, Jane M. *The Psychology of the Female Body.* London: Routledge, 1989.

Vankeep, P. A. "Childfree Cheer." In *Human Behavior* 4 (1975): 44.

Veevers, Jean E. "The Childfree Alternative: Rejection of the Motherhood Mystique." In *Women in Canada,* ed. M. Stephenson. Toronto: New Press, 1973.

———. "The Life Style of Voluntarily Childless Couples." In *The Canadian Family in Comparative Perspective.* Ontario: Prentice Hall of Canada, 1976.

———. "Voluntary Childless Wives: An Exploratory Study." *Sociology and Social Research* 57 (1973): 356–66.

Voell, Paula. "For Her It was Love, Marriage, Family." In *The Buffalo News,* 12 April 1987, Sec. F, p. 1.

Wattenberg, Ben. *The Birth Dearth.* New York: Pharos Books, 1987.

Weedon, Chris. *Feminist Practice and Poststructural Theory.* New York: Basil Blackwell, 1987.

Wilk, Carole A. *Career Women and Childbearing: A Psychological Analysis of the Decision Process.* New York: Van Nostrand Reinhold Company, 1986.

INDEX